Personal development:

50 BESTSELLERS IN INFOGRAPHICS

CONTENT:

1   **The Willpower Instinct.**
How Self-Control Works, Why It Matters, and What You Can
Do To Get More of It   6
Joseph O'Connor, Ian McDermott

2   **Grit: The Power of Passion and Perseverance**   8
Joseph O'Connor, Ian McDermott

3   **Performance: The Secrets of Successful Behaviour**   10
Robin Stuart-Kotze

4   **The Obstacle is the Way. The Timeless Art of Turning Trials into Triumph**   12
Ryan Holiday

5   **Managing Performance: Performance Management in Action**   14
Michael Armstrong, Angela Baron

6   **Execution: The Discipline of Getting Things Done**   16
Larry Bossidy, Ram Charan

7   **Mini Habits: Smaller Habits, Bigger Results**   18
Stephen Guise

8   **The Brain That Changes Itself: Stories of Personal Triumph
from the Frontiers of Brain Science**   20
Norman Doidge

9   **Thinking, Fast and Slow**   22
Daniel Kahneman

10   **The Art of Systems Thinking: Essential Skills for Creativity
and Problem Solving**   24
Joseph O'Connor, Ian McDermott

11   **Accidental Genius: Using Writing to Generate
Your Best Ideas, Insight, and Content**   26
Mark Levy

12   **What Got You Here Won't Get You There: How Successful
People Become Even More Successful**   28
Marshall Goldsmith, Mark Reiter

13   **The Black Swan: The Impact of the Highly Improbable**   30
Nassim Taleb

| 14 | **The Future of the Mind: The Scientific Quest to Understand, Enhance, and Empower the Mind**
Michio Kaku | 32 |

| 15 | **Flow: The Psychology of Optimal Experience**
Mihaly Csikszentmihalyi | 34 |

| 16 | **Emotional Intelligence: Why It Could Matter More Than IQ**
Daniel Goleman | 36 |

| 17 | **Search Inside Yourself: The Unexpected Path to Achieving Success, Happiness (and World Peace)**
Chade-Meng Tan | 38 |

| 18 | **Mindset. The New Psychology of Success. How We Can Learn to Fulfill Our Potential**
Carol Dweck | 40 |

| 19 | **Letting Go: The Pathway of Surrender**
David Hawkins | 42 |

| 20 | **Thanks for the Feedback: The Science and Art of Receiving Feedback Well**
Douglas Stone, Sheila Heen | 44 |

| 21 | **Emergent Strategy: Shaping Change, Changing Worlds**
Adrienne Brown | 46 |

| 22 | **Everything is Negotiable! How to Get the Best Deal Every Time**
Gavin Kennedy | 48 |

| 23 | **A Complaint is a Gift: Using Customer Feedback As a Strategic Tool**
Janelle Barlow, Klaus Moeller | 50 |

| 24 | **Influencer: The Power to Change Anything**
Kerry Patterson, Joseph Grenny, David Maxfield, Ron McMillan, Al Switzler | 52 |

| 25 | **The Leader Who Had No Title: A Modern Fable on Real Success in Business and in Life**
Robin Sharma | 54 |

| 26 | **The Innovator's DNA: Mastering the Five Skills of Disruptive Innovators**
Jeff Dyer, Hal Gregersen, Clayton Christensen | 56 |

CONTENT:

27	**Tribal Leadership: Leveraging Natural Groups to Build a Thriving Organization** *Dave Logan, John King, Halee Fischer-Wright*	58
28	**Good to Great: Why Some Companies Make the Leap… and Others Don't** *Jim Collins*	60
29	**Principles: Life and Work** *Ray Dalio*	62
30	**Leading The Leaders: How To Enrich Your Style of Management and Handle People Whose Style Is Different From Yours** *Ichak Adizes*	64
31	**Great by Choice: Uncertainty, Chaos and Luck — Why Some Thrive Despite Them All** *Jim Collins, Morten Hansen*	66
32	**Great People Decisions: Why They Matter So Much, Why They Are So Hard, and How You Can Master Them** *Claudio Fernández-Aráoz*	68
33	**Reinventing Organizations** *Frederic Laloux*	70
34	**My Years with General Motors** *Alfred Sloan*	72
35	**The Fifth Discipline. The Art & Practice of the Learning Organization** *Peter Senge*	74
36	**Chasing the Rabbit: How Market Leaders Outdistance the Competition and How Great Companies Can Catch Up and Win** *Steven Spear*	76
37	**Creativity, Inc.: Overcoming the Unseen Forces That Stand in the Way of True Inspiration** *Amy Wallace, Edwin Catmull*	78
38	**How The Mighty Fall: And Why Some Companies Never Give In** *Jim Collins*	80

| 39 | **The Dance of Change: The Challenges to Sustaining Momentum in a Learning Organization**
Peter Senge, George Roth | 82 |
| 40 | **The Goal: A Process of Ongoing Improvement**
Eliyahu Goldratt, Jeff Cox | 84 |
| 41 | **How Google Works**
Eric Schmidt, Jonathan Rosenberg | 86 |
| 42 | **The Tiredness Cure. How to Beat Fatigue and Feel Great for Good**
Sohere Roked | 88 |
| 43 | **Why Zebras Don't Get Ulcers: The Acclaimed Guide to Stress, Stress-Related Diseases, and Coping**
Robert Sapolsky | 90 |
| 44 | **How to Stay Sane**
Philippa Perry | 92 |
| 45 | **The Power of Full Engagement. Managing Energy, Not Time, Is the Key to High Performance and Personal Renewal**
Jim Loehr, Tony Schwartz | 94 |
| 46 | **The Blue Zones: Lessons for Living Longer From the People Who've Lived the Longest**
Dan Buettner | 96 |
| 47 | **Full Catastrophe Living: Using the Wisdom of Your Body and Mind to Face Stress, Pain, and Illness**
Jon Kabatt-Zinn | 98 |
| 48 | **How not to Die. Discover the Foods Scientifically Proven to Prevent and Reverse Disease**
Michael Greger | 100 |
| 49 | **The Telomere Effect: A Revolutionary Approach to Living Younger, Healthier, Longer**
Elizabeth Blackburn, Elissa Epel | 102 |
| 50 | **The Oxygen Advantage: Simple, Scientifically Proven Breathing Techniques to Help You Become Healthier, Slimmer, Faster, and Fitter**
Patrick McKeown | 104 |

The Willpower Instinct. How Self-Control Works, Why It Matters, and What You Can Do To Get More of It

Kelly McGonigal

1. **Look after your health:** be active in sports, get enough sleep, do breathing exercises, eat healthful food, meditate, find time for religious and spiritual practices, and enjoy quality time with friends and family to help boost your willpower resources.

2. **Don't try to control and improve all your thoughts, desires and actions simultaneously.** Make small steps towards your goal, set intermediate goals and celebrate your achievements (especially when you are doing something you don't really enjoy).

3. **Don't become obsessed with a task and don't suppress your doubts, negative thoughts and emotions.** Just observe and accept them.

4. **Start with minor things, like watching your posture,** staying away from sweets, and controlling the time you spend on the internet. Try to do something new every day.

5. **If there are items on your to-do list that you frequently postpone,** change their periodicity, frequency, or repetition, not the desired behavior.

6. **Learn to foresee where and when you may break your promise.** Apply the 10-minute rule: contain yourself for 10 minutes before you give in to a temptation. Meanwhile, recall your goal and distance yourself from the temptation (at least turn away).

7. **If you suffer a lapse, don't lash out at yourself,** instead forgive and encourage yourself, as you would do with a close friend.

8. **Look for a "new tribe", surround yourself with like-minded people** who do the same things as you do, and who strive for the same goals. Act as a team.

9. **Devote several minutes** at the start of each day to thinking about your plans.

10. **Remember your goals and promises.**

The Willpower Instinct

Kelly McGonigal

Your willpower is just a part of the brainwork that can be trained as a muscle.

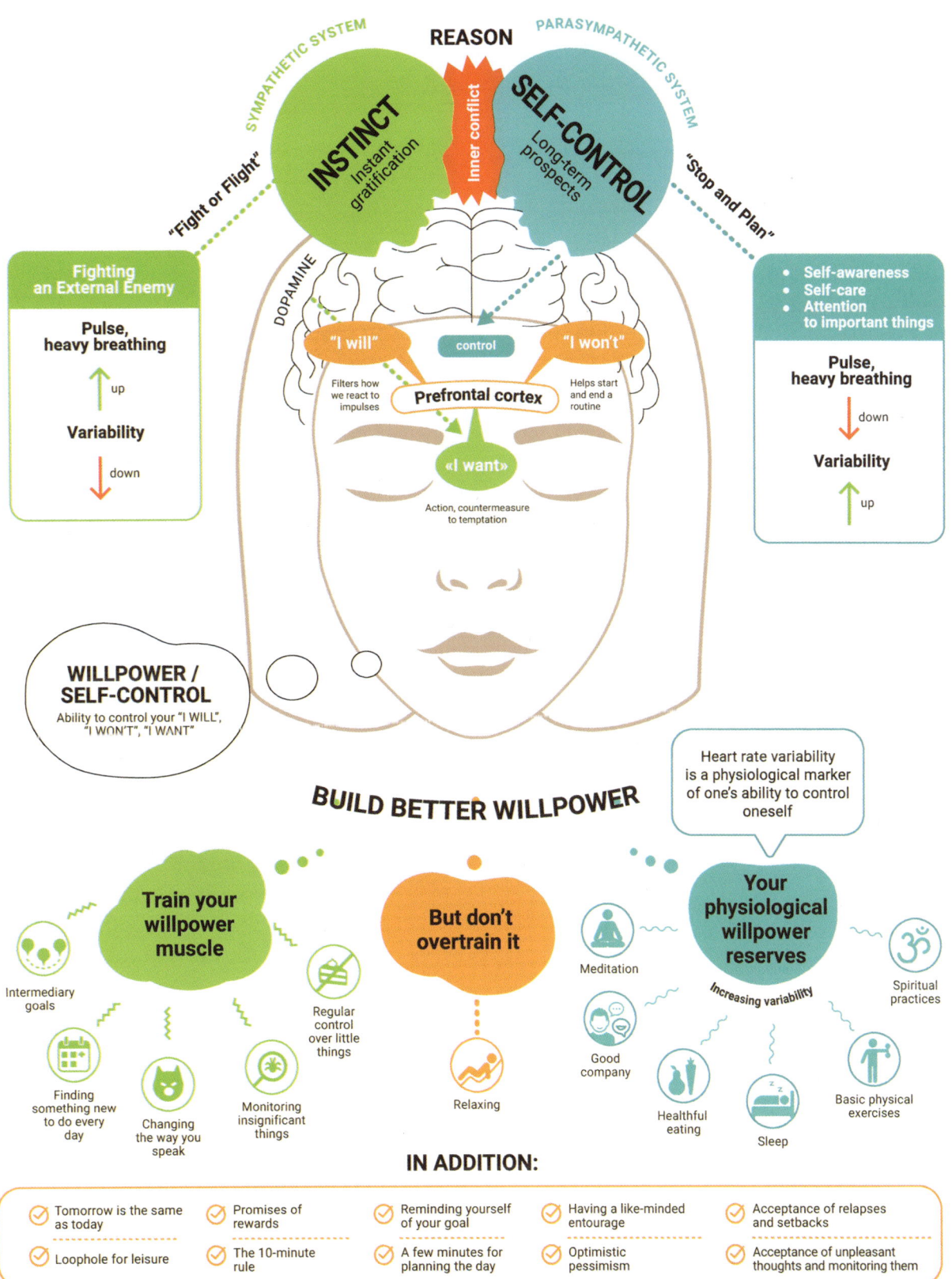

Personal development: 50 bestsellers in infographics

Grit: The Power of Passion and Perseverance

Angela Duckworth

1 **Our success in life largely depends on our perseverance in attaining long-term goals.** Natural abilities play a much smaller part.

2 **There are four pillars supporting grit:** interest, practice, purpose, and hope.

3 **Interest is not an automatic.** One needs to seek, develop and take possession of an interest proactively.

4 **True mastery = talent × hard work.** Great achievements = mastery × hard work. Unlike talent, hard work is present in both equations.

5 **The deliberate practice method envisages discovering an area to work on,** focusing your attention on what you are doing, and getting feedback from people whose opinion matters to you.

6 **Having a clear hierarchy of goals will help you find your calling and will allow you to acquire and preserve your passion.** Goals can be:
1) top-level (just one in every aspect of life),
2) medium-level (they serve to respond to the intermediary question of "why?"), or
3) low-level (tasks that, if completed, move you closer to attaining medium-level goals.

7 **A global goal is always connected to the people around you.** You will find your calling when you discover how your work contributes to the well-being of others.

8 **Believing that through effort you can improve your future** and focusing on development will give you strength to survive tough times.

9 **If you want to develop grit from the inside out, develop and expand your interests.** Set high goals, try to outperform yourself. Try to have an optimistic worldview and treat challenges as opportunities. A cognitive psychologist may assist you with acquiring an optimistic worldview.

10 **Use external help to develop grit outside-in.** Parents, teachers, trainers, coaches, bosses and friends are there to support you in a time of need and help you to soldier on when you're ready to throw in the towel.

Grit

Angela Duckworth

Talent and innate ability alone don't predict success. It is a special combination of passion and perseverance, which Angela Lee Duckworth refers to as grit, that is a strong predictor of high achievement.

SUCCESS FACTORS

Ability to work things through and overcome your challenges even if don't always succeed

Craving for becoming a better version of yourself, desire to learn and hone our skills all the time

INTEREST

Discover, develop, sustain

- Consider what things you regard as really important.
- Try different things to have a better understanding as to whether your assumptions about your interests correspond to reality.
- After you have discovered an interest, don't let the situation develop by itself. Gain knowledge, find a coach.
- Seek novelty in the details. Expand your knowledge network and hone your skills.

PRACTICE

Get better by practicing as hard as possible

- Focus on your weakness: development isn't possible without ricing to the challenge.
- Go all out to attain your goal.
- Seek feedback and don't be afraid of criticism.
- Analyze your iterations.

GRIT

HOPE

Expect that your efforts will improve your future and develop a growth mindset

- Reconsider your notions of intelligence and talent.
- Try to develop an optimistic worldview.
- Ask for help, find a mentor.

PURPOSE

Treat your job as if it your calling

- Spend some time thinking how your job contributes to the well-being of others.
- Find a role model and get inspired.
- Discover a way to put your job in line with your values.

Performance: The Secrets of Successful Behaviour

Robin Stuart-Kotze

1. **Less than 10% of the variance in a person's behavior is explained by personality.** 90% is driven by the circumstances that define the person's winning strategy.

2. **Performance is primarily driven by a person's behavior, not his or her personality.** Behavior is what needs to be improved.

3. **In an ever-changing world, it is impossible to choose the best form of behavior for all circumstances.** If you believe that you're performing to the best of your abilities, you're most likely falling behind. You need stay on top of yourself all the time. The questions you need to answer are: "Is everything being done in the best possible way?" "What can I do to perform at an even higher level?"

4. **Change is only possible when an individual or members of a team have decided to change.** In order to get it started, one must accept both the good and the bad of his or her current behavior.

5. **The person who best knows how to enhance performance in a particular job is the one doing the actual job.**

6. **People are more likely to accept their own ideas and reject those originating from others.** In order to change people's behavior, ask them to think of ways to do something more efficiently as opposed to simply handing down strict instructions.

7. **Measurable and verifiable data are prerequisites for success.** You will be working haphazardly if data are not verifiable.

8. **Leadership is not a characteristic with which a person is born.** It can and must be learned. The components of strong leadership are: focusing on tasks, building and maintaining relationships, coordinating activities, being able to set up an integrated process and result system, and having a global outlook.

9. **Adverse behavior is contagious.** It not only impedes our reaching our goals, it also places unnecessary pressure on the people involved and discourages and humiliates them. It curtails performance and usually comes as a reaction to stress or the result of a person having chosen the wrong career.

10. **An efficient team consists of 8–10 people who have the same goal.** Horizontal ties within it are just as important as vertical ones.

Performance

Robin Stuart-Kotze

BLOCKING BEHAVIOR −

- Negative reaction to external stimuli
- Stands in the way of reaching targets

Impacting Factors
- Humiliation
- Stress
- Lack of self-confidence
- Anxiety
- Fear of losing

Behavior Types
- **Protective aggression** — Animosity towards peers and direct reports
- **Deflection** — Shifting responsibility onto others
- **Avoidance** — Keeping silent, not speaking up

Outcomes:
- Demotivation
- Energy drain
- Lack of initiative

✓ ACCELERATING BEHAVIOR

Leadership
- Beyond titles or ranks
- Leadership behavior can be acquired

Motivation
- Internal gratification
- Proper workload distribution
- Trust in management

Team
- Consists of 8–10 people
- Has the same goal
- Has a leader that
  - steers them toward their goal
  - sets individual key productivity indicators
  - keep tabs on members
  - acts as a role model
  - has teammates' backs

Organization structure
- Horizontal ties are no less important than vertical ties

Values
- Defined by actions, not words
- Manifested in personnel's behavior
- Backed up by team unity
- Not necessarily the same as customer values

PERFORMANCE is primarily driven by a person's behavior, not his or her personality, and a person's behavior is something he or she can control

↓
BEHAVIOR
↑ ↑
CONTROL   CHANGE

PERFORMANCE IMPROVEMENT PRINCIPLES

PEOPLE CHANGE THEIR BEHAVIOR ONLY WHEN THEY BECOME AWARE THAT CHANGE IS REQUIRED

Performance is driven by behavior

Work must be relevant

Come to terms with your current behavior

The people who actually do the job know it best

The one who initiates the change steers it

Ask, don't give instructions

Measure data

Personal development: 50 bestsellers in infographics

The Obstacle is the Way.
The Timeless Art of Turning Trials into Triumph

Ryan Holiday

1. **The world is not perfect, and it does not owe us anything.** It is unpredictable, and it places obstacles in our way. Wisdom ensues when we regard these obstacles as opportunities.

2. **Benefit can be drawn from any obstacle,** as this makes us stronger, gives us valuable experience, helps us get to know ourselves better, teaches us to focus our efforts on the right track, and when one road dead ends, it opens a multitude of others.

3. **The many success stories of great people show us that obstacles are essential for progress.**

4. **Turning shortfalls into triumphs requires learning three disciplines:** perception, action, and will.

5. **When you face an obstacle, practice objectivity, control your emotions and focus on what can be done.** Try to realize that no crisis will last forever, and any error you make is just a blip on the map.

6. **Do not succumb to the general panic.** Think outside the box and look for a way out where nobody else expects to find it.

7. **Get going.** Use any opportunity to get something done. We will be and will do many things in our lives. None are beneath us. Be energetic, persistent and pragmatic.

8. **True will, which must be both inculcated and then cultivated,** is humility and the ability to accept the inevitable.

9. **Hope for the best but prepare for the worst.** Always have a worst-case scenario on hand.

10. **Learn to accept what you cannot fight and enjoy your surroundings.** Be grateful for what you have. Accept your mortality. Offer your help to other people in their time of need.

The Obstacle is the Way

Ryan Holiday

What we can do is not just succeed against all odds, but turn obstacles into opportunities so that what stands in our way becomes the actual way forward.

ACTION

Get going, make the first step.

Practice persistence.

Channel your energy.

It hurts to fail, but there will be no better teacher.

Follow the process, focus on the smallest task you have right now.

Any job you do, do it right.

Be pragmatic, think progress, not perfection.

Be creative in your approach, application, maintain your sense of humor.

What matters is not what just happened, but what you plan on doing about it next.

PERCEPTION

Practice objectivity, control your emotions.

Alter your perception.

Focus on what is in your power.

Live in the present moment.

Don't follow others, have your doubts, ask questions.

Look at opportunities hiding behind obstacles.

Recognize your strengths.

It's up to you to decide what you feel in a specific situation.

WILL

Build your inner fortress: a sound mind is a sound body.

Be able to give in and accept what can't be changed.

Be prepared for hard times.

There are benefits in everything, learn to see them.

Be persistent and resilient in progressing towards your goal.

Become stronger by helping others.

We are mortal: learn to cherish life.

Be prepared to start anew.

True will is quiet humility, any other type of will is weakness and blind ambition.

Managing Performance: Performance Management in Action

Michael Armstrong, Angela Baron

1 **Performance management is a necessary component of any organization's management system.** That said, there is no single template applicable to every organization.

2 **The performance management cycle consists of four processes: planning, action, monitoring, and review.** Their sequence may vary.

3 **Qualitative performance measures are as important as quantitative ones.**

4 **Poor performance often results from poor skills and insufficient motivation on the staff level.** However, management failures may also play a part.

5 **Performance planning consists of three stages:** setting the direction, concluding performance agreements, and agreeing personal development plans.

6 **Financial indicators, output, impact, reaction, and time are important measures for monitoring performance.**

7 **Performance management is an ongoing process, but formal review meetings are needed once or twice a year.** Review meetings help reinforce motivation, create comfortable labor conditions, improve communication and rank staff objectively on the basis of performance.

8 **Feedback on performance should be immediate, built into operating procedures, and fact-based.** It should address specific actions and events, not personality.

9 **When you evaluate results, measure them against agreed targets only.**

10 **A rating helps measure an individual's input into the overall result.** It is recommended to use a four-level rating scale that does not have a totally negative level ("outstanding," "efficient," "developing," "meeting basic requirements").

Managing Performance

Michael Armstrong, Angela Baron

Efficient performance management takes into account the interests of every employee, provides for freedom of labor and development, and encourages cooperation.

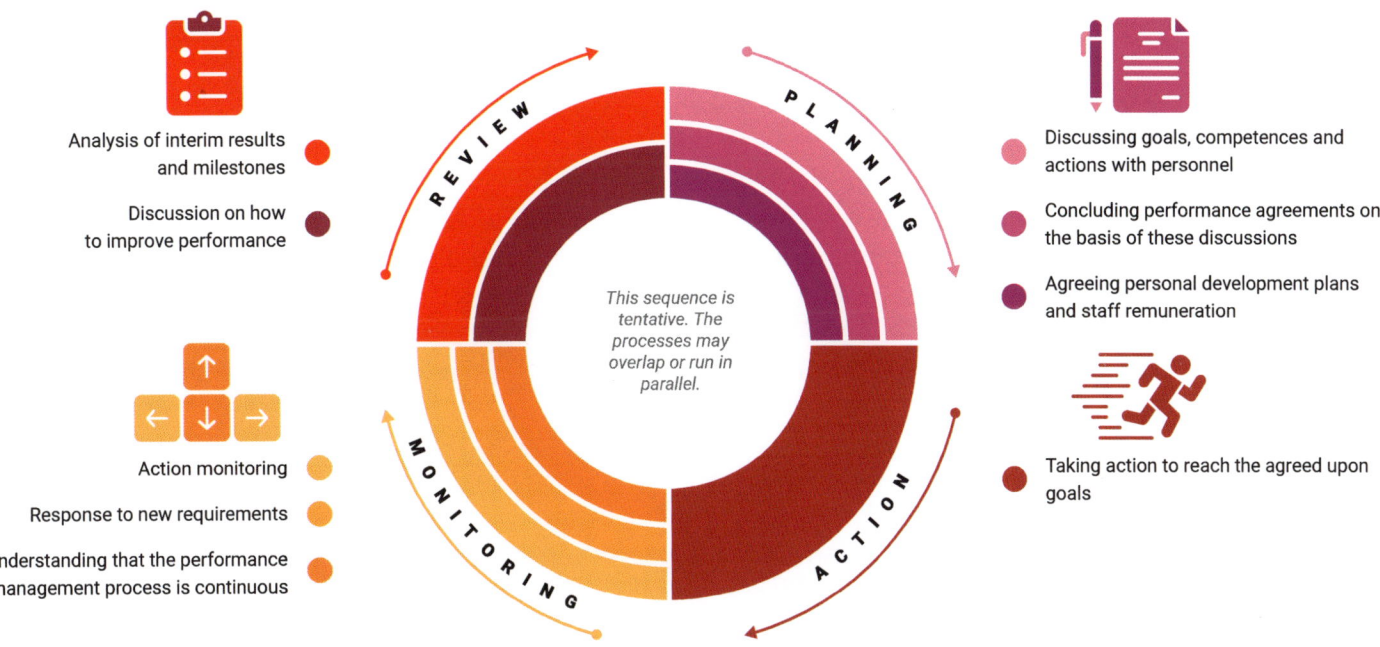

- Analysis of interim results and milestones
- Discussion on how to improve performance

- Discussing goals, competences and actions with personnel
- Concluding performance agreements on the basis of these discussions
- Agreeing personal development plans and staff remuneration

- Action monitoring
- Response to new requirements
- Understanding that the performance management process is continuous

- Taking action to reach the agreed upon goals

This sequence is tentative. The processes may overlap or run in parallel.

PERFORMANCE MEASURES

Personnel and management should agree on them during the planning process

1. **FINANCE** — Income | profit | added value | costs
2. **OUTPUT** — Units produced or processed | sales | new accounts
3. **IMPACT** — Reach quality standards | boost demand | complete the project
4. **REACTION** — Feedback from colleagues and external customers
5. **TIME** — Period between order placement and completion | number of delays

REVIEW MEETINGS

The goal is to discuss an individual's achievements and agree future plans (to be held 1-2 times a year

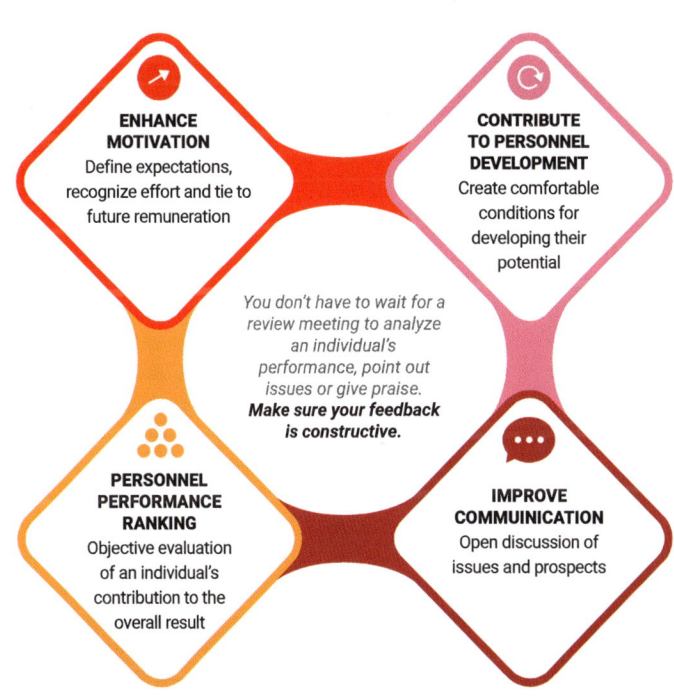

- **ENHANCE MOTIVATION** — Define expectations, recognize effort and tie to future remuneration
- **CONTRIBUTE TO PERSONNEL DEVELOPMENT** — Create comfortable conditions for developing their potential
- **PERSONNEL PERFORMANCE RANKING** — Objective evaluation of an individual's contribution to the overall result
- **IMPROVE COMMUNICATION** — Open discussion of issues and prospects

You don't have to wait for a review meeting to analyze an individual's performance, point out issues or give praise. **Make sure your feedback is constructive.**

Execution: The Discipline of Getting Things Done

Larry Bossidy, Ram Charan

1. **Execution-driven management** is a system focused on getting things done.

2. **The core competencies of a proper manager** are authenticity, self-awareness, self-mastery, and humility.

3. **An execution culture is focused on three core processes:** the people process, the strategy process, and the operation process.

4. **The strategy process** defines where a business wants to go.

5. **The people process** defines who is going to get it there.

6. **The operation process** provides the path for these people.

7. **Leaders of successful businesses know all the processes inside out,** they can be objective in evaluating the company's position compared to the competition, and they're good at identifying weaknesses.

8. **Cultural change starts** when personnel begin understanding the company's goals.

9. **If a staff member fails to deliver, he or she should be trained, moved to a different position or terminated.** If a staff member is efficient, he or she should be rewarded, including monetarily.

10. **When you are building your operational plan, focus on the desired outcome.** Discuss collectively all proposals and assumptions on which the plan is based, and then devise a system for effective collaboration.

The Discipline of Getting Things Done

Larry Bossidy, Ram Charan

Bright CEOs, talented personnel, a great strategy... Why are results below par? Oftentimes the reason why a business fails to deliver on its promises is that it has no operational management system.

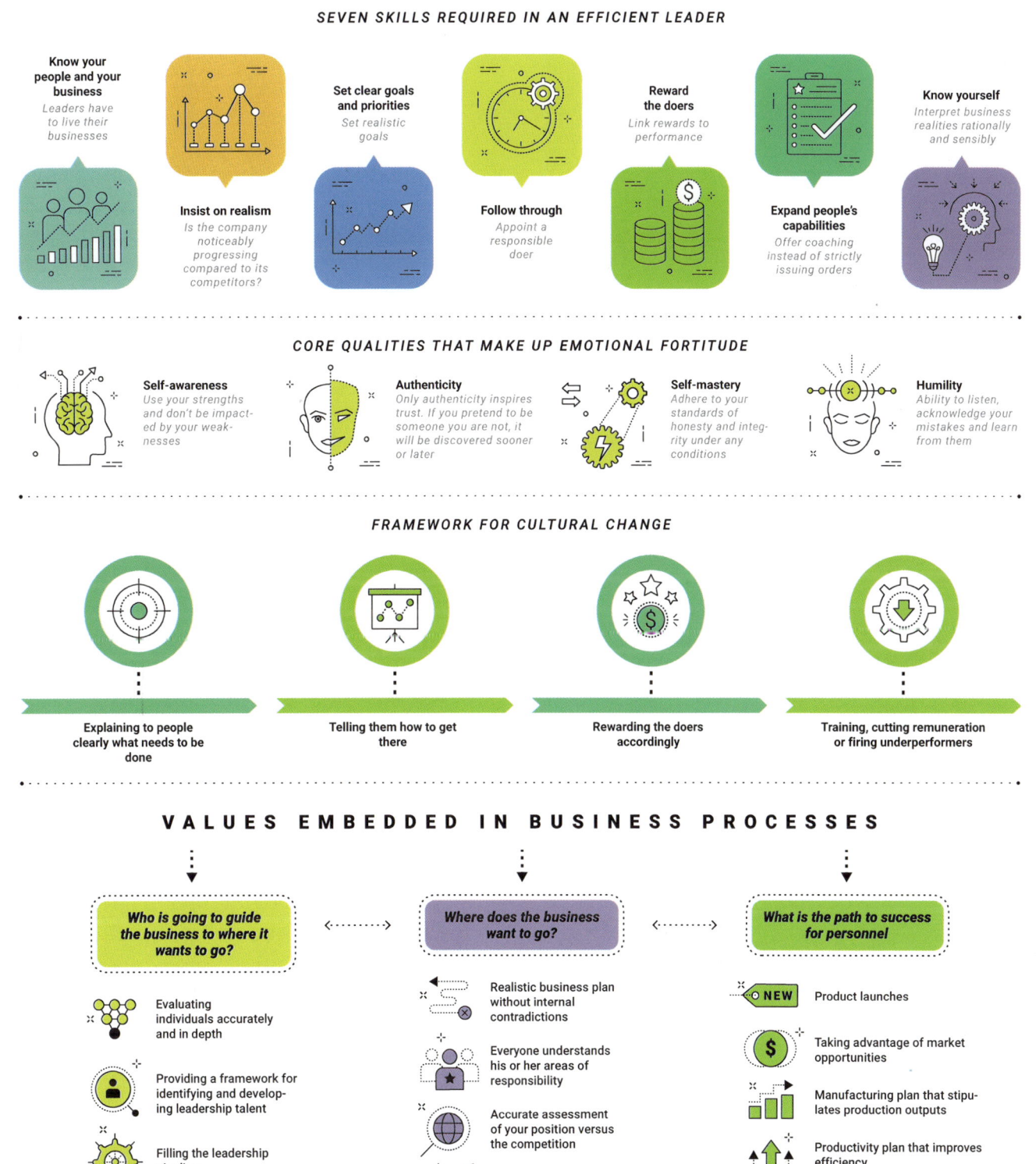

SEVEN SKILLS REQUIRED IN AN EFFICIENT LEADER

- **Know your people and your business** — Leaders have to live their businesses
- **Insist on realism** — Is the company noticeably progressing compared to its competitors?
- **Set clear goals and priorities** — Set realistic goals
- **Follow through** — Appoint a responsible doer
- **Reward the doers** — Link rewards to performance
- **Expand people's capabilities** — Offer coaching instead of strictly issuing orders
- **Know yourself** — Interpret business realities rationally and sensibly

CORE QUALITIES THAT MAKE UP EMOTIONAL FORTITUDE

- **Self-awareness** — Use your strengths and don't be impacted by your weaknesses
- **Authenticity** — Only authenticity inspires trust. If you pretend to be someone you are not, it will be discovered sooner or later
- **Self-mastery** — Adhere to your standards of honesty and integrity under any conditions
- **Humility** — Ability to listen, acknowledge your mistakes and learn from them

FRAMEWORK FOR CULTURAL CHANGE

1. Explaining to people clearly what needs to be done
2. Telling them how to get there
3. Rewarding the doers accordingly
4. Training, cutting remuneration or firing underperformers

VALUES EMBEDDED IN BUSINESS PROCESSES

Who is going to guide the business to where it wants to go?
- Evaluating individuals accurately and in depth
- Providing a framework for identifying and developing leadership talent
- Filling the leadership pipeline

Where does the business want to go?
- Realistic business plan without internal contradictions
- Everyone understands his or her areas of responsibility
- Accurate assessment of your position versus the competition
- Resource allocation in proportion to opportunities

What is the path to success for personnel
- Product launches
- Taking advantage of market opportunities
- Manufacturing plan that stipulates production outputs
- Productivity plan that improves efficiency
- Clear contingency plan for force majeure circumstances

Personal development: 50 bestsellers in infographics

Mini Habits: Smaller Habits, Bigger Results

Stephen Guise

1. **Most popular growth strategies don't work** because they suggest that you act against yourself and your brain, which by nature is slow to adapt change and prefers stability.

2. **The Mini Habit strategy** is forcing yourself to abandon massive goals in favor of actually doing things and getting results.

3. **A mini habit is a very small version of a larger positive behavior, but one that can fit in extremely tight schedules.** Its core function is to get the ball rolling.

4. **By doing tiny steps every day, you change your habitual mindset,** create an endless positive feedback loop, grow to believe in yourself and develop a superior habit-building strategy.

5. **Motivation is unreliable because it requires constant support and a lot of energy.** It begins to fade as soon as a behavior becomes a habit.

6. **Willpower is limited.** If you don't want your endeavor to fail, your tasks should not be too complicated or too difficult and should not bring about negative emotions, while your energy levels must also be sufficient.

7. **It should be easy to start and to make further steps.** It's important that your brain not begin resisting change. Doing a little bit is better than doing nothing at all. Doing a little bit every day has a greater impact than doing a lot on a particular day.

8. **Mini-habits reinforce your self-confidence** and teach you to be brave so you can make your first steps in a new direction, which is the perfect foundation for personal growth.

9. **Start with developing one mini-habit that requires not more than 10 minutes a day.** Review your progress and mood in seven days and adjust the habit or add another one. If you feel inner resistance, it is better to make the task easier. The most important thing is doing something every day.

10. **Write down your progress, reward yourself for each achievement, and get rid of your high expectations.**

Mini Habits

Stephen Guise

Stephen Guise proposes breaking down major tasks into very small steps that don't exhaust one's willpower or spirit but rather help the person make constant forward progress.

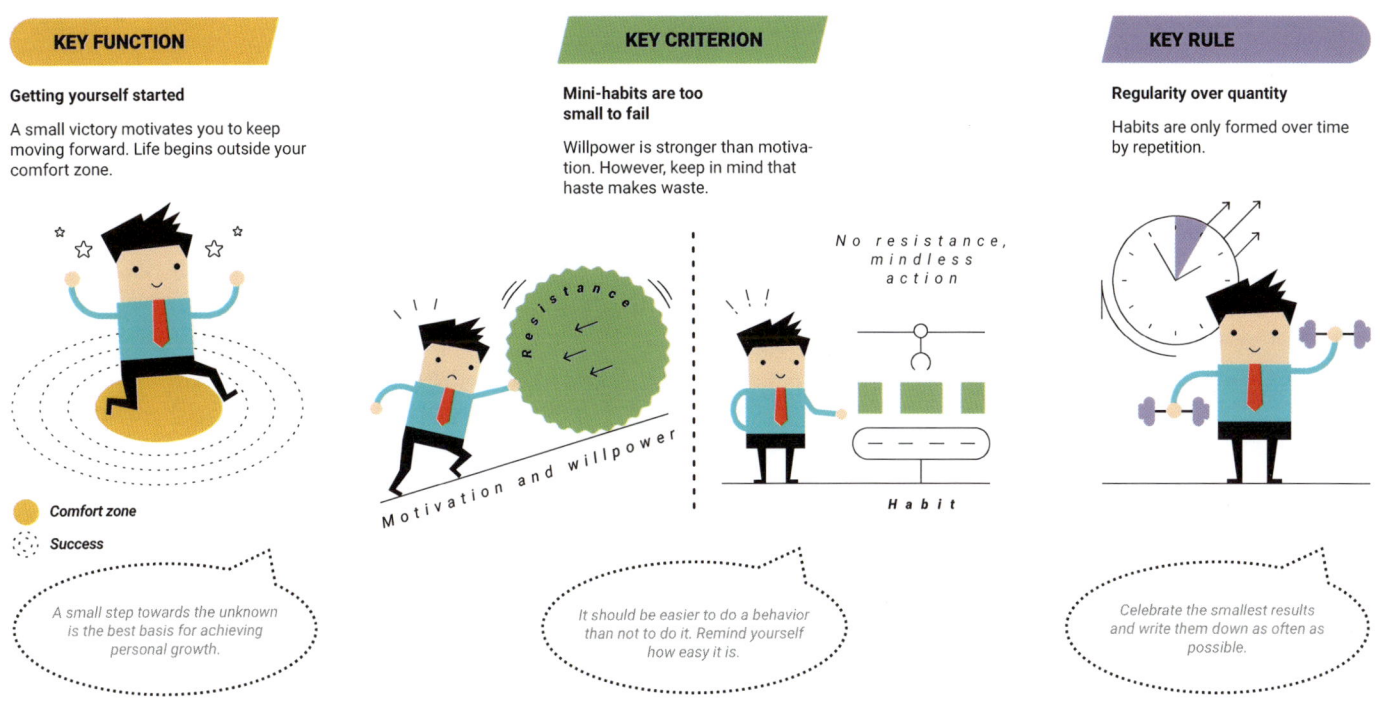

KEY FUNCTION

Getting yourself started

A small victory motivates you to keep moving forward. Life begins outside your comfort zone.

- Comfort zone
- Success

A small step towards the unknown is the best basis for achieving personal growth.

KEY CRITERION

Mini-habits are too small to fail

Willpower is stronger than motivation. However, keep in mind that haste makes waste.

It should be easier to do a behavior than not to do it. Remind yourself how easy it is.

KEY RULE

Regularity over quantity

Habits are only formed over time by repetition.

Celebrate the smallest results and write them down as often as possible.

EIGHT SMALL STEPS TO BIG CHANGE

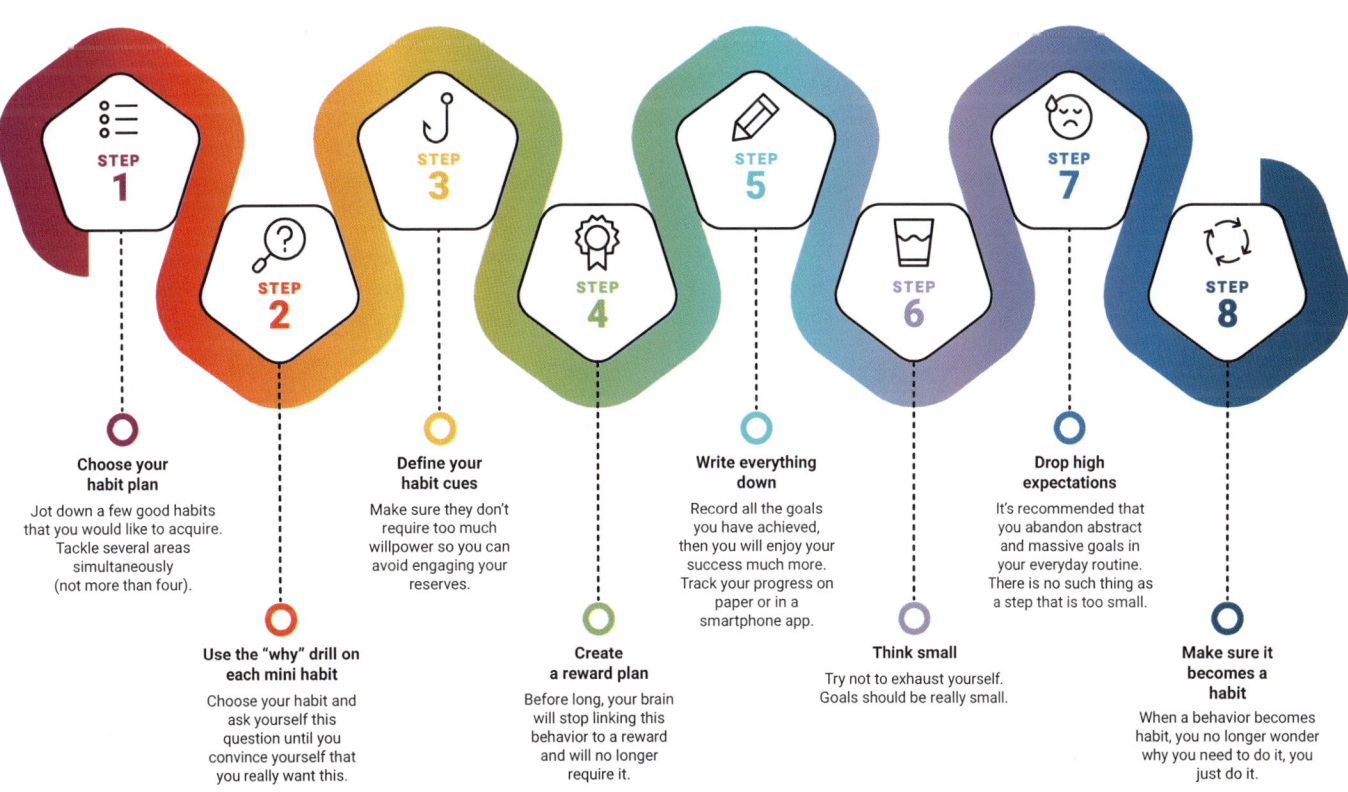

STEP 1 — Choose your habit plan
Jot down a few good habits that you would like to acquire. Tackle several areas simultaneously (not more than four).

STEP 2 — Use the "why" drill on each mini habit
Choose your habit and ask yourself this question until you convince yourself that you really want this.

STEP 3 — Define your habit cues
Make sure they don't require too much willpower so you can avoid engaging your reserves.

STEP 4 — Create a reward plan
Before long, your brain will stop linking this behavior to a reward and will no longer require it.

STEP 5 — Write everything down
Record all the goals you have achieved, then you will enjoy your success much more. Track your progress on paper or in a smartphone app.

STEP 6 — Think small
Try not to exhaust yourself. Goals should be really small.

STEP 7 — Drop high expectations
It's recommended that you abandon abstract and massive goals in your everyday routine. There is no such thing as a step that is too small.

STEP 8 — Make sure it becomes a habit
When a behavior becomes habit, you no longer wonder why you need to do it, you just do it.

Personal development: 50 bestsellers in infographics

The Brain That Changes Itself: Stories of Personal Triumph from the Frontiers of Brain Science

Norman Doidge

1. **Whatever you do in real life, or in your imagination, it has a physical impact on your brain.** The brain changes every second of every day.

2. **For as long as you live, your brain will be able to rearrange itself by forming new neuron connections.**

3. **The more you practice a skill, the easier it becomes for you.** Your neurons learn as you learn.

4. **Damaged or dysfunctional brain cells and neuron circuits can regenerate and reprogram themselves.**

5. **Brain injuries are not irreversible!** Stimulation exercises can help restore many, if not all, brain functions.

6. **In order to function properly, the brain needs sufficient sleep, healthful food and a minimum of stressful consequences,** which can be achieved by implementing exercise and breathing exercises.

7. **By practicing a skill, you change millions, even billions of neural circuits.** When we learn, we not only acquire new knowledge, but also we also change the brain's structure, improving its capacity and plasticity.

8. **The brain follows a simple pattern: if something is not put to good use, it becomes redundant.** Each bad habit gradually gets more control over the brain's map and prevents this space from being used to form good habits.

9. **Try to avoid multitasking when you work or study.** Long-lasting changes to the brain can only occur when you are truly focused on what you are doing.

10. **Studying foreign languages, mastering a new craft, or solving simple mathematical problems can keep the brain healthy and delay its ageing by 20–30 years.**

The Brain That Changes Itself

Norman Doidge

The brain can change and heal itself throughout your lifetime. Neuroplastic miracles require no injections or surgeries; just willpower and hard work.

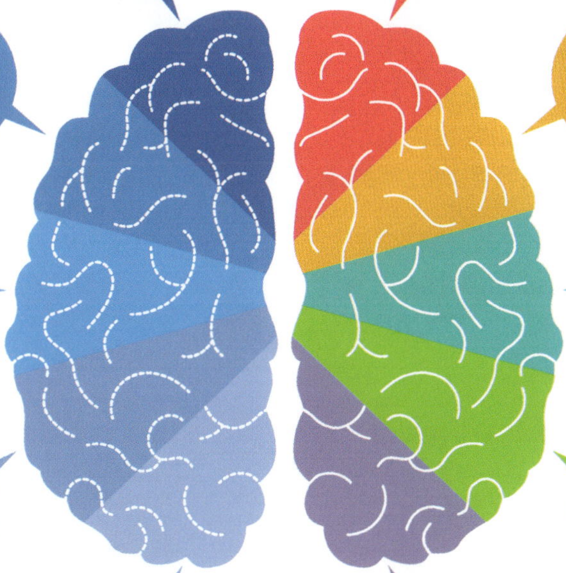

You're confined to your desk all day long
A sedentary lifestyle disrupts the blood supply to the brain

Your diet includes a lot of simple carbohydrates
White flour, sugar, etc.

You live in chronic stress
As a response to stress, the brain reduces hippocampus, and this can result in memory impairment

You don't get enough sleep
Lack of sleep results in concentration issues and memory impairment

You devote a lot of time to gadgets
Your attention becomes fragmented

You are active in sports
Sports stimulate neuron growth, which, in turn, improves learning abilities

You adhere to a healthful diet
Seafood such as salmon, mackerel, or Atlantic herring are especially good for proper brain functioning

You cope with stress
using flexibility and breathing exercises and meditation

You sleep at least 7-8 hours a day
Sleep quality is as important as its duration

You do a lot of things that require focused attention
This includes reading advanced books, studying foreign languages, etc.

TIPS TO IMPROVE MEMORY AND SPEED OF THOUGHT

When we learn, we don't just acquire new knowledge, but also change the brain's structure and improve its learning abilities.

1. A strong signal produces a bigger impact on the brain
If you want to memorize something, the incoming signal should be clear

2. If you're practicing a skill, let it have all your attention
You should be fully engaged

3. Exercise your brain by exposing it to something it's not used to
A new way home, new dances, new tastes of food, or new scents

4. Try your daily routine at a different pace or with a different hand
For example, clean your teeth using your left hand, not the habitual right one

5. Engage other senses in a habitual situation
Watch a movie in mute mode, trying to read the actors' lips, or dine in absolute darkness

Personal development: 50 bestsellers in infographics

Thinking, Fast and Slow

Daniel Kahneman

1. **There are two modes of thought:** intuitive (fast and spontaneous) and deliberate (slow and conscious).

2. **Fast thinking is automatic, instinctive and effortless.** It produces impressions and emptions and controls a lot of what you do.

3. **Slow thinking is conscious, effortful, logical and calculating.** It monitors and controls thoughts and actions suggested by your fast thinking.

4. **Deliberate thinking is much too slow for making routine decisions.** The best we can do is compromise: learn to recognize situations in which mistakes are likely and engage slow thinking when the stakes are high.

5. **People often make mistakes when they are tired or when their slow thinking is engaged in something else.** What's more, people are heavily influenced by first impressions and the availability effect (we perceive easily available data as more reliable and accurate).

6. **People overestimate the probability of unlikely events** and place too much emphasis on unlikely events in their decisions because they naturally focus on all things unusual.

7. **If a satisfactory answer to a hard question is not found quickly, then quick thinking will find a related question that is easier and will answer it instead.** Make sure you're don't fall victim to such substitutions when making your final decision.

8. **Having experienced an unexpected event, we often change our outlook on life to adapt to a new situation.** When a new world landscape is completed, the old one gets erased, and a person can't remember what he or she once believed.

9. **A person will have a hard time telling the truth from a lie if the latter is "somewhat familiar" to him.** Lies often seem to be true if they have a logical or associative connection to other convictions that we have or come from a course we have a connection to.

10. **Paying close attention during an activity can improve the outcome in many situations.** It is especially important when we make comparisons, or choose or provide a rationale for something.

Thinking, Fast and Slow

Daniel Kahneman

Our fast, intuitive thinking is prone to be overconfident, make radical hypotheses and build unrealistic plans. By using slow, effortful thinking, we can learn to recognize the situations in which mistakes are likely.

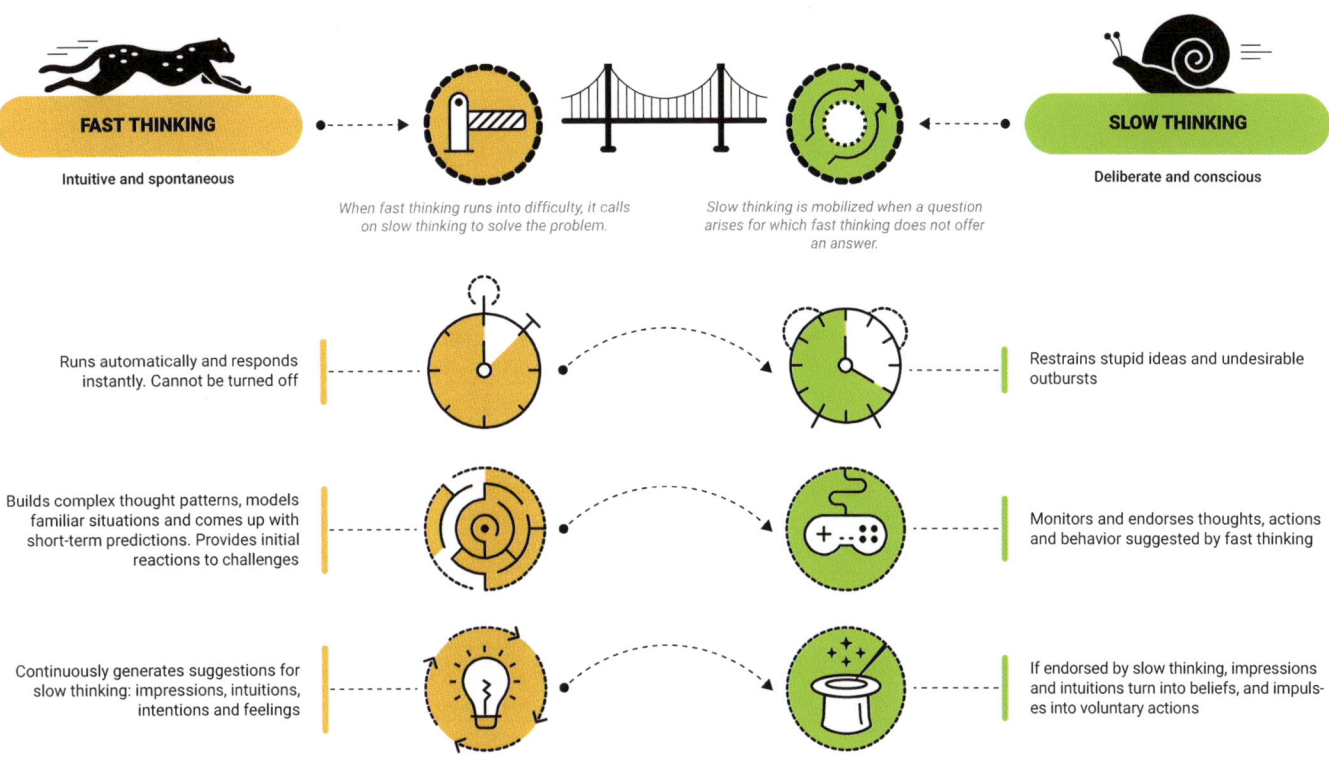

TIPS TO MINIMIZE MISTAKES

Personal development: 50 bestsellers in infographics

The Art of Systems Thinking: Essential Skills for Creativity and Problem Solving

Joseph O'Connor, Ian McDermott

1) A system is something that maintains its existence and functions as a whole through the interaction of its parts. Systems thinking looks at the whole, and the parts, and the connections between them.

2) Emergent properties of a system are those that materialize from the system while it is working. The only way to find out how a system functions is to see it in action

3) It is the relationship and the mutual influence between the individual parts that is important, rather than the number or size of the parts. It is when we detect common principles that we begin to understand the properties of various systems, even those that may seem chaotic at a first glance.

4) There is a limit to how big a system can grow. At a certain point it will become unwieldy, hard to manage and more prone to breaking down. In a business or organization, it makes sense to divide big systems into smaller ones.

5) A system works as well as its weakest link. When you try to improve a system by increasing the efficiency of just one of its parts, the system loses its balance.

6) Complex systems are attracted to stability. Changing a system requires:
1) finding the weakest part and focusing on it, or
2) destabilizing the system and creating a new stabilization state to which the system should aspire.

7) Systems thinking is thinking in loops rather than in straight lines. Feedback is fundamental in systems as it can be reinforcing (changes in the whole system feed back to amplify the original change) or balancing (changes in the whole system feed back to oppose the original change). Feedback often comes with time delays.

8) The world is illogical and chaotic and systems, being cyclical, involve factors of time and recursion (feedback received from smaller problems originating from the same problem). Therefore, to understand the process, formal logic of "cause - effect - stop" is not enough.

9) Our mental models are also systems, and they allow us to see just parts of the whole. This narrows our world.

10) Systems thinking makes it possible to break out of the circle of stereotypes, have a better understanding of the situation and people, and widen our mental models.

The Art of Systems Thinking

Joseph O'Connor, Ian McDermott

The book explains how systems thinking helps us build business models, organizations and human relations. More importantly, it teaches us a different way of thinking outside mental models and subjective views.

SYSTEM

A SYSTEM IS SOMETHING THAT MAINTAINS ITS EXISTENCE AND FUNCTIONS AS A WHOLE THROUGH INTERACTION OF ITS PARTS.

PROPERTIES
Systems thinking looks at the whole, and the parts, and the connections between the parts.

• • •

Emergent properties only emerge from the system as a whole.

• • •

If you take a TV set apart, you will hardly be able to watch your favorite movie.

SYSTEM COMPLEXITIES
Detail complexity means there is a great number of different parts (jigsaw puzzle).

• • •

Dynamic complexity means there is a great number of possible connections between the parts, because each part may have a number of different states (chess).

• • •

The more connections you have, the more influence you can exercise.

MENTAL MODELS
Mental models are like filters through which we see the world: assumptions, ideas and value systems.

• • •

Systems thinking that uses both objective and subjective views makes it possible to break out of the circle of stereotypes and have a better understanding of the situation and other people.

LEVERAGE
In order to change a complex system, you need to find it weakest part and focus effort on this very part. This is called the leverage principle.

• • •

When pressure for change builds up in a system, it can suddenly burst like a balloon. It only takes a small trigger to make it collapse.

• • •

The demolition of the Berlin Wall and the breakup of the Soviet Union are good examples.

THINKING IN CIRCLES
Systems thinking is thinking in loops rather than straight lines. Feedback is fundamental in systems.

• • •

When a system's output is then returned to the source but in a modified way, thereby producing a different result, this is called a feedback loop.

• • •

When you receive a response from a person you are in a conversation with, his or her words can influence what you will say next.

CAUSE AND EFFECT

FALLACY 1
The effect ALWAYS comes after the cause

The formal logic of cause — effect — stop rarely works in systems, as the cause may be the effect, and vice versa.

The chicken or the egg: which came first?

FALLACY 2
Effect follows cause CLOSELY in time and space

There is often a time delay factor in systems, and an effect may occur far away in time and space from its cause.

When you have back pains, a doctor checks your heart and appendix, not just your spine.

FALLACY 3
The effect is PROPORTIONAL to the cause

When influence is exercised on living organisms, this is not always correct.

A tiny virus could kill an entire village some centuries ago.

LEARNING IS CHANGING OURSELVES USING THE FEEDBACK FROM OUR ACTIONS

WHAT PREVENTS US FROM LEARNING?

01 Ignoring part of the feedback, deleting part of the information.

02 The dynamic complexity of systems, which prevents us from understanding them, or a significant time delay between the cause and effect.

03 Limiting mental models, not paying attention to feedback from our senses.

04 Difficulties in measuring feedback. (If a person is not crying, it does not mean that he or she is not hurting.)

05 Setting thresholds for feedback that are either too high or too low.

06 Our inability to ask the right questions.

Accidental Genius: Using Writing to Generate Your Best Ideas, Insight, and Content

Mark Levy

1. **Freewriting allows you to put to work the knowledge stored in your mind, as well as analyze, develop and then apply it in a deliverate manner.** This process produces revelations and breakthrough ideas.

2. **Thoughts are fleeting.** They may be trivial, valuable, or extremely valuable. Jot down your thoughts so you can sort the wheat from the chaff. This method works if you write with a time limit, write continuously, and write at the speed of thought.

3. **There are efficient methods that help you set your mind free, teach you to improvise, and change your views.** For example, it is necessary to separate two independent freewriting processes: writing and analyzing your writing.

4. **A freewriting session starts with "leads", which are unfinished sentences you write down to "download" your mind on a piece of paper.** The more thoughts, the better. One thought develops the other. You're exploring various points of view.

5. **If you're stuck, try playing with your imagination.** Imagine you're writing a letter to somebody else. You can try describing an imaginary dialogue with a friend. Prompt your thinking by asking questions.

6. **Freewriting makes you more attentive to routine events.**

7. **In order to accomplish very important tasks, consider doing a writing marathon of 20-minute sessions, alternating freewriting with editing your text.** Keep this marathon going for several hours. When a person gets tired, he discovers his own super-abilities.

8. **Freewriting is not just writing for yourself, this material can generate articles, blog posts, or even books.**

9. **The ability to focus on the most important things helps you achieve more in life.**

10. **There is never a dead end.** People, situations and opinions change. You always have some leeway. Fill it up with thoughts that lead to a better life.

Accidental Genius

Mark Levy

Freewriting is a skill that allows you to put to work the knowledge stored in your mind, as well as analyze, develop and then apply it in a deliverate manner.

FREEWRITING PRINCIPLES

WRITE RAPIDLY AND CONTINUOUSLY
- Write at the speed of thought
- Take no phone calls and answer no emails
- Separate writing and revising

WORK WITH A TIME LIMIT
- Define a short, finite period for writing continuously
- Consider doing marathons of 20-minute writing sessions that add up to hours

WRITE THE WAY YOU THINK
- Jot down everything that comes to your mind, don't worry about logic or grammar
- Get inspired by the routine
- Explore, invent, and jot down ideas
- Come up with a collection of thoughts: jot things down without trying to evaluate them

TRY EASY
- Force your internal editor into a subservient role, so you can get to raw thoughts
- Start with "leads" (incomplete phrases like, "I remember how...," or "I want to know about..."
- Jot down simple facts, they help see a new solution

REDIRECT YOUR ATTENTION
- Ask yourself simple questions, provide reasoning for your opinion
- Look at the situation from a different perspective
- Transform texts into articles, blog posts, or books
- Practice idea breeding

GO WITH THE THOUGHT
- Agree with what you've just written, and logically extend it
- Jot down questions; it's easier than coming up with solutions right off the bat
- Record imaginary dialogues, assume the role of your imaginary partner
- Use your imagination: conscious playing with fictitious narratives opens un new possibilities

FREEWRITING BENEFITS

- It clears logjams in your mind.
- It helps you generate fresh and original ideas.
- It enables you to use the power of your mind for achieving your goals outside writing.
- It prompts your mind to think more widely, deeply, and differently than your peers.

Personal development: 50 bestsellers in infographics

What Got You Here Won't Get You There: How Successful People Become Even More Successful

Marshall Goldsmith, Mark Reiter

1. **People who have already reached a certain level of success tend to take on bad habits,** which prevent them from seeing possibilities and developing further.

2. **When success comes, we tend to overestimate our contribution to our endeavor,** take credit for successes that truly belong to others, develop an elevated opinion of our professional skills, and conveniently ignore the costly failures and time-consuming dead ends we have created.

3. **Professional skills of successful people are usually above par,** while their communication skills often leave much to be desired.

4. **Some bad habits result from arrogance and self-indulgence,** while others are a consequence of emotional immaturity and disrespect for people.

5. **Being obsessively goal-oriented can prevent us from achieving success.** We go all in without truly understanding what we want and what others want from us.

6. **People are often not opposed to changing their behavior, but they tend to put off these changes because of "how busy they are."** You will never find the best time for change. Start changing now.

7. **Obtaining honest, confidential feedback from partners, colleagues,** and competitors is crucial to understanding what a person needs to change.

8. **Once you have committed to change, it is important to understand what needs to be changed first.** Then attack this issue, while not trying to achieve absolute perfection.

9. **Goals should be clear and specific.** If you can measure it, you can achieve it.

10. **Money is among the most efficient the most efficient drivers of change.**

What Got You Here Won't Get You There

Marshall Goldsmith, Mark Reiter

People who have already reached a certain level of success tend to acquire short-sited convictions and bad habits, which prevent them from seeing possibilities and developing further.

20 Habits That Stand in the Way of Success

1. Being too concerned about winning
2. Always having to be involved in everything
3. Needing to evaluate people and impose your opinion on them
4. Making destructive, sarcasitc, and caustic comments
5. Overusing "no," "but" or "nevertheless"
6. Always displaying their superior intellect
7. Using their emotional instability
8. Needing to sow the seeds of doubt, "don't say I didn't warn you."
9. Withholding information to maintain their advantage
10. Failing to recognize and encourage people
11. Taking credit from something they didn't do
12. Tendency to make excuses
13. Passing blame on events and people from the past
14. Protecting their favorites
15. Refusing to apologize and admit mistakes
16. Intentionally ignoring people to show them disrespect
17. Failing to express gratitude
18. Punishing the innocent who simply wanted to help
19. Passing the buck
20. Excessive pride in themselves

Beliefs That Prevent Actual Change

I have succeeded
A poll has revealed that 80-85% of respondents rate themselves in the top 20% of their peer group - and 70% rate themselves in the top 10%.

I can succeed
"I am successful, and I do things my way and this leads me to success" (misconception).

I will succeed
There's a risk of overestimating your strengths and not knowing when to stop.

I choose to succeed
Lack of flexibility may be a limiting factor for successful people.

Rules That Help Leaders Change

Feedback is crucial to understanding what a person needs to change

Make sure you need to change

Pick the right area

Don't be delusional about what you truly need to change

Don't hide from the truth

There is no perfect behavior

If you can measure it, you can achieve it

Monetize your results

The best time for change is now

Personal development: 50 bestsellers in infographics

The Black Swan: The Impact of the Highly Improbable

Nassim Taleb

1. **A Black Swan is a highly improbable event that has a massive impact on our world.** Many Black Swans become known as such because no one saw them coming. Fashion, ideas, religions, historical events, etc., all follow these Black Swan dynamics.

2. **In hindsight, it is not difficult to identify the role of Black Swans, but predicting them is impossible.** Therefore, we should rely less on planning and focus more on improvisation and recognizing opportunities when they present themselves.

3. **People tend to discuss Black Swans they can grasp and ignore the ones that don't fit into their patterns.** The Black Swans that we discuss and fear are totally different from the Black Swans that can actually place us in danger.

4. **The aggregate of all scalable phenomena form a Mediocristan.** It consists of natural phenomena and people doing "regular" jobs. On the contrary, Extremistan is a multitude of non-scalable social phenomena and the "habitat" of researchers, authors, stock market speculators, who may gain enormous advantages thanks to a Black Swan.

5. **In order to succeed and gain exposure to positive Black Swans,** you should learn to live in a state of uncertainty, stop striving for high-level accuracy, and be open to the emergence of your lucky chance.

6. **People tend to make forecast errors, overstate their capabilities and understate risk, especially if they were successful in avoiding risk in the past.**

7. **Stay away from detailed governmental plans and don't rely on large-scale forecasts.** A vast array of big numbers can often intoxicate people.

8. **If you want to figure out the nature of success, you should also study failures.** Success stories often fail to show you the full picture.

9. **Learn to differentiate between positive Black Swans and negative Black Swans.** Use all opportunites availabe to you. Don't get caught in a routine, have more contact with people. Chances of being exposed to a positive Black Swan are higher in the city than in a scarcely populated rural area.

10. **Think outside the box and don't try to predict your exposure to a specific Black Swan.** Focus on the consequences that you can foresee.

The Black Swan

Nassim Taleb

A Black Swan is a highly improbable event that carries a massive impact and consequences.

MAJOR DELUSIONS

- Focus on the known, not on the whole picture
- Assuming the past is a sound body of evidence for forecasting the future
- Focus on a narrow range of Black Swans, disregarding other events
- Matching a narrative or pattern to a series of facts
- Accumulation of confirmatory observations
- There are no Black Swans

Drawing the wrong conclusion

WE DO NOT KNOW WHAT WE HAVE YET TO LEARN

MEDIOCRISTAN
THE AGGREGATE OF SCALABLE PHENOMENA

EXTREMISTAN
THE AGGREGATE OF NONSCALABLE PHENOMENA

Mediocristan	Method	Extremistan
Events are distributed according to the Gaussian bell curve. **Consistent knowledge, accumulation**	Method	Distribution according to the exponential Pareto curve. **Just one decisive observation or extraordinary event**
Stability, predictability, consistency, planning, experience, physical quantities	Keywords	Risk, competition, inequality, numbers, income, extreme events
Get a small segment of the total pie	Winners	Take it all
In our ancestral environment	More likely to be found	In our modern environment
Low	Black Swan emergence probability	High

Mediocre Members: Doctors, teachers, workers

Dwarfs and Giants: Stockbrokers, researchers, authors

THE ROAD TO EXTREMISTAN

Black Swans emerge exactly because nobody expects them

1. Accept that "accidents" may happen
2. Don't get caught up in trying to know the cause
3. Stay away from large-scale projects and governmental plans
4. Focus on consequences
5. Bear in mind that one-sided forecasts may be erroneous
6. Learn to identify "accidents"
7. Study failures, not only success stories

Personal development: 50 bestsellers in infographics

The Future of the Mind: The Scientific Quest to Understand, Enhance, and Empower the Mind

Michio Kaku

1. **The human brain has 100 billion neurons that form sophisticated neural networks.** It weighs about 1.5 kg (2% of the body's mass), works even when we sleep, and consumes 20% of our energy. Once the brain dies, the host dies as well.

2. **Brain studies did not begin until the mid-19th Century.**

3. **By the end of the 19th Century, it was established that various areas of the brain had their own "focus",** that the right cerebral hemisphere controlled the left side of the body, while the right side was controlled by the left cerebral hemisphere.

4. **In the 1930s researchers established a connection between brain cortex areas and the organs they control.** The more complex organ functions are, the larger the respective cortex area is.

5. **The oldest part of the brain developed about 500 million years ago.** It is responsible for basic biological functions such as breathing, digestion, heartbeat, mating, food gathering, fighting, etc. Because this part of the brain is similar to that of a reptile, it is called the reptilian brain.

6. **The second oldest brain system is the limbic brain.** This is where emotions are born, memories are stored, and body temperature is regulated. It is also where sensory data on hunger, thirst, pleasure and stresses are collected and distributed.

7. **The neocortex, which is the prefrontal brain area, is responsible for cognitive behavior.** It accounts for 80% of human brain weight. Some animals also have a neocortex. The neocortex is smooth in rodents, whereas in humans it is convoluted.

8. **The prefrontal cortex is responsible for rational decisions, the right parietal lobe is in charge of sensory perception and integration, and the left parietal lobe is in charge of fine movements and specific aspects speech.** The occipital lobe perceives and processes visual information, while the temporal lobe recognizes faces and emotions.

9. **A true revolution in human brain studies occurred about 20 years ago, when the MRI scanner was invented.**

10. **In order to be comparable to the human brain, artificial intelligence must learn to recognize images and develop common sense.**

The Future of the Mind

Michio Kaku

The human brain is the most complex item in the Universe, and artificial intelligence has only reached the insect level so far. In order to be on par with the human brain, it must learn to recognize images and develop common sense.

 **Reptilian Brain** — In charge of core body functions  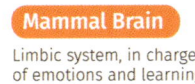 **Mammal Brain** — Limbic system, in charge of emotions and learning  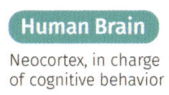 **Human Brain** — Neocortex, in charge of cognitive behavior

BRAIN AND NEOCORTEX (OUTER CEREBRUM LAYER)

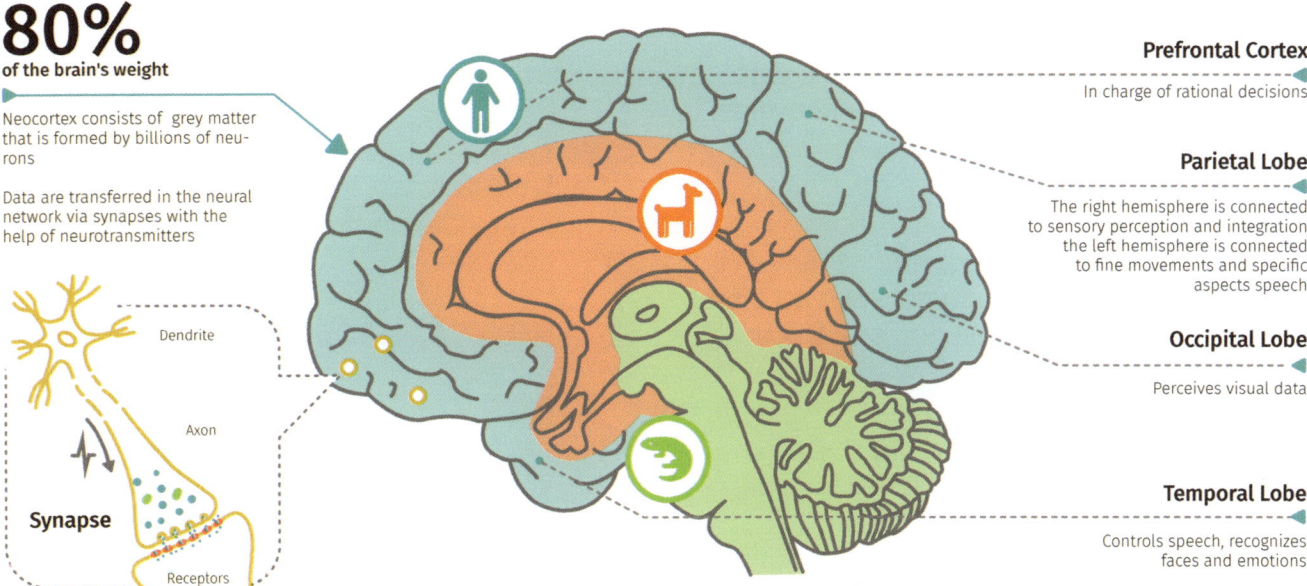

80% of the brain's weight

Neocortex consists of grey matter that is formed by billions of neurons

Data are transferred in the neural network via synapses with the help of neurotransmitters

Prefrontal Cortex — In charge of rational decisions

Parietal Lobe — The right hemisphere is connected to sensory perception and integration the left hemisphere is connected to fine movements and specific aspects speech

Occipital Lobe — Perceives visual data

Temporal Lobe — Controls speech, recognizes faces and emotions

PRESENT-DAY METHODS FOR STUDYING AND AFFECTING THE BRAIN

 Magnetic Resonance Imaging (MRI) — An MRI scanner allows us to monitor the thought process. The method has contributed to progress in the study of mental disorders and strokes

 Transcranial Electrical Stimulation (TES) — Anesthesia without medicines, mental health and cardiovascular performance recovery, drug addiction treatment

 Magnetoencephalography (MEG) — Diagnostics of autoimmune and mental conditions, ability to localize epileptic focuses

THE FUTURE OF THE HUMAN BRAIN

 **Healthcare** — Treatment of extremely serious conditions and injuries; Artificial brain areas; Neuroprosthetics

 **Intelligence enhancement** — Medicines to stimulate intelligence; Gene modification; Instrumental brain stimulation

 **Mind reading and object control** — Telepathic helmets; Nanoprobes; Controlled avatars

 **Image recognition** ... **THE FUTURE OF ARTIFICIAL INTELLIGENCE** ... 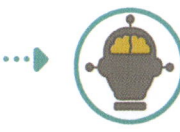 **Development of common sense**

Personal development: 50 bestsellers in infographics

Flow: The Psychology of Optimal Experience

Mihaly Csikszentmihalyi

1. **Happiness is essentially the ability to control your emotional experiences.**

2. **A self-sufficient individual** is one who can find purpose in life and his activities, is resolute and lives in harmony.

3. **Flow is the antidote to the disorder of the mind.** When we experience flow, we are fully immersed in an activity and enjoy it, while gaining confidence and the ability to reach higher heights.

4. **Satisfaction does not bring happiness,** but it helps us obtain inner orderliness.

5. **Happiness is impossible without clear goals and immediate feedback.**

6. **A person's undertakings should be commensurate with his abilities.** Activity as such does not bring a sense of accomplishment.

7. **Bodily needs (food, sex) can be transformed into flow experiences** if they are controlled and made more complex.

8. **People with higher intelligence are happier than those with lower intelligence.** To become happier work on developing your memory, read, improve your speech, do research, and study history.

9. **A job can provide opportunities for flow.** If we reject passively getting through the workday, our jobs can always be made more enjoyable if we learn new skills and set achievable goals.

10. **Gregariousness is important for experiencing happiness,** but until a person learns to live in isolation and enjoy it, he or she will have difficulty solving matters that demand complete concentration.

Flow

Mihaly Csikszentmihalyi

Attention is our most important tool for improving the quality of our experience, or flow, which leads to joy and happiness.

Happiness is not the result of good fortune or random chance. It does not depend on outside events, but rather on how we interpret them.

The most important step in becoming free from the controls of society is to develop the ability to enjoy the here and now.

We cannot reach happiness by consciously striving to achieve. We experience it only by being fully immersed in every detail of our lives.

Happiness is a state that must be cultivated and preserved from within.

Our body and all our senses can be a source of optimal experience:

- Awareness of your body in motion: taking a walk, gardening, playing catch with a child
- Food, if you are conscious of what you eat and can differentiate the flavors of various dishes
- Appreciate the visual, art, nature
- Conscious immersion into music

A job can provide opportunities for flow:

- When optimal experience takes place, people become so involved in what they are doing that the activity becomes spontaneous, almost automatic; they stop being aware of themselves as separate from the actions they are performing
- Regardless of the kind of job, the tasks a person faces should be achievable
- A job should resemble team sports and always be a challenge that requires developing your skills
- A job will be enjoyable when the one doing it assumes responsibility for its better organization

People of flow can transform their harrowing conditions into a field of study and behave themselves as if they are experiencing flow

- They pay close attention to the most minute details of their environment and discover in it hidden opportunities for action
- They set goals appropriate to their situation and closely monitor progress
- They up the ante, setting increasingly complex challenges
- They assert control over their situation by finding a new direction for their psychic energy

People of flow have one thing in common: they seek something meaningful that that they place above their own interests

How can one learn to experience flow:

- Set goals and monitor feedback
- Become immersed in your activity
- Pay attention to what is happening around you
- Learn to enjoy the here and now

By setting personal development as your ultimate goal, you can make your life a continuous flow experience.

Emotional Intelligence: Why It Could Matter More Than IQ

Daniel Goleman

1. **Emotions are a crucial element in any decision making.** That is why emotional intelligence is just as important for becoming successful as academic intelligence, which we express as IQ.

2. **Emotional intelligence cannot be measured or tested by linear methods,** but its level can be evaluated by a person's behavior.

3. **Emotional intelligence manifests itself in a person's ability to regulate his or her emotions** and maintain a positive mindset even when facing a stressful situation.

4. **Negative emotions such as anger, fear, or sadness are the most difficult to control.** This requires a high level of emotional intelligence.

5. **Flow, or the aggregate of all the best manifestations of both emotional and academic intelligence (IQ),** is the best state of mind for a person to have when working.

6. **Social intelligence, which is the ability to influence other people's emotions, is extremely important for a leader.** One of the best ways to manifest this talent is by providing constructive feedback.

7. **For a couple, emotional intelligence means being able to interact constructively,** show empathy, and make a conscious effort to maintain a thoughtful relationship.

8. **Positive emotions generate energy to fight illnessesillnesses.** A positive mindset can have a positive impact on a person's physical health.

9. **Parents are responsible for the emotional intelligence of their small children.** If parents have a rapport with and help their child deal with emotions, the child gradually learns to identify and regulate emotion and develops advanced emotional intelligence by the time he or she reaches maturity.

10. **Emotional intelligence can be developed at any age by making a conscious effort to do so, or with the assistance of professionals.**

Emotional Intelligence

Daniel Goleman

Daniel Goleman's book is a study into our second intellect, emotional intelligence, which is just as essential to the thought process as the thinking rational brain.

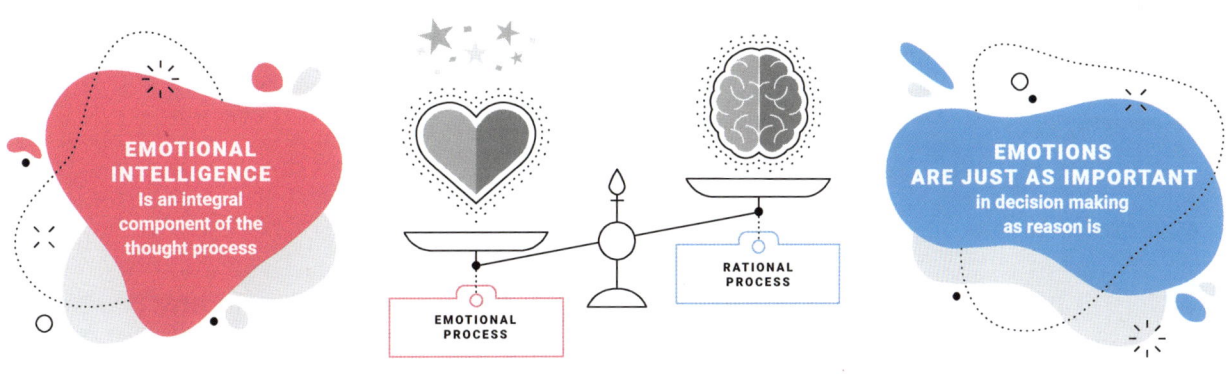

EMOTIONAL INTELLIGENCE Is an integral component of the thought process

EMOTIONS ARE JUST AS IMPORTANT in decision making as reason is

EMOTIONAL INTELLIGENCE COMPONENTS

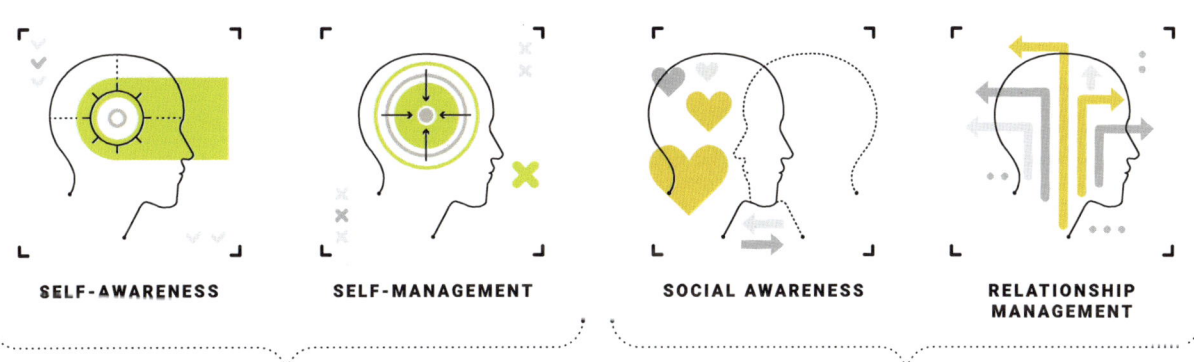

SELF-AWARENESS   **SELF-MANAGEMENT**   **SOCIAL AWARENESS**   **RELATIONSHIP MANAGEMENT**

INSIDE

WHAT DO I FEEL?
Anger, fear, love, sadness, happiness...

SELF-AWARENESS
Staying impartial and retaining analytical skills in a raging sea of emotions

POSITIVE MOTIVATION
Ability to motivate oneself to stay on course

PERFORMANCE AND ANXIETY
A modicum of nerves propels outstanding achievements

HOPE AND OPTIMISM
Having a strong expectation that things will turn out all right in life, and believing in your ability to make it happen

INSPIRATION
Being able to enter flow is emotional intelligence at its best

OUTSIDE

SOCIAL OR INTERPERSONAL SKILLS:

TEAM BUILDING
Showing initiative and coordinating team efforts

DISCUSSING DECISIONS
Talent for mediation, conflict prevention or settlement

PERSONAL CONNECTION
Talent for empathy and network building

SOCIAL ANALYSIS
Being able to detect and have insights about people's feelings, motives and concerns.

SOCIAL INTELLIGENCE and each of its components can be developed by making a conscious effort

Personal development: 50 bestsellers in infographics

Search Inside Yourself: The Unexpected Path to Achieving Success, Happiness (and World Peace)

Chade-Meng Tan

1. **Peace and happiness can ultimately spread around the world if everyone has inner peace.** This is achievable if you develop your emotional intelligence.

2. **The development of emotional intelligence consists of three steps:** attention and concentration training; self-knowledge; and, the creation of useful mental habits.

3. **Emotional intelligence creates conditions for stellar success at work,** strong leadership and personal success, which is why people with EI are always successful.

4. **Emotional intelligence consists of five domains.** The first one is self-awareness, and there are three emotional competencies under this domain: emotional awareness, accurate self-assessment, and self-confidence.

5. **Emotional intelligence development starts with training your attention through meditation.** It is not some mystic ritual, but rather a set of mental exercises that the brain needs just like the body needs physical exercises.

6. **You can meditate in any posture you find comfortable and that helps you remain alert and relaxed at the same time.** This state of mindfulness can improve your understanding of other people and make you enjoy life more.

7. **Self-regulation means managing one's internal actions and reactions.** It is not about avoiding painful emotions, but rather avoiding their denial or repression.

8. **Self-motivation refers to emotional tendencies that guide or facilitate reaching our goals.** The best way to find motivation at work is to find your higher purpose. When that happens, our work can become a source of sustainable happiness for us.

9. **Empathy is awareness of the feelings, needs and, concerns of others.** Empathy increases with kindness and perceived similarity.

10. **Social skills serve to induce desirable responses in others.** Crucial social skills are compassionate leadership, influencing with goodness, and communicating with insight.

Search Inside Yourself

Chade-Meng Tan

Chade-Meng Tan, whose business card introduces him as "the jolly good fellow of Google", has devoted himself to creating conditions for world peace. He believes this can be achieved through spreading inner peace and developing emotional intelligence.

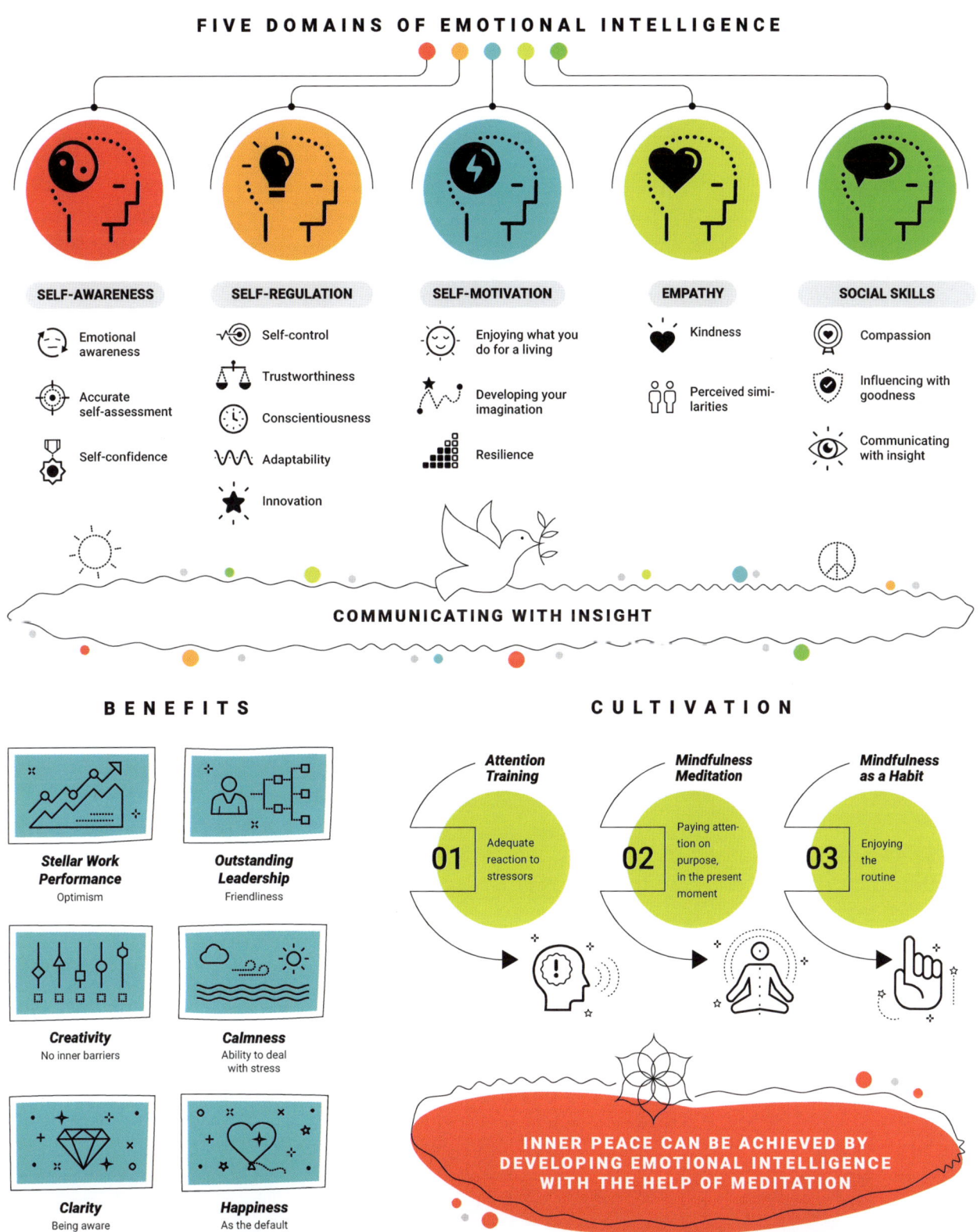

Personal development: 50 bestsellers in infographics

Mindset. The New Psychology of Success. How We Can Learn to Fulfill Our Potential

Carol Dweck

1. **Success in school, work, sports and personal relations can be dramatically influenced by how we think about our talents and aptitudes.**

2. **People with a "fixed" mindset believe that abilities are innate and stay the same during their lifetime.** Every situation calls for a confirmation of their intelligence, personality, or character. They strive for control and excellence, otherwise they lose interest.

3. **People with a "growth" mindset believe that what you are dealt with is just the starting point for development, and your basic qualities are things you can cultivate through your efforts, your strategies, and help from others.** They love taking risks and confronting challenges.

4. **The "growth" mindset helps a person excel in just about anything in life.** Many growth-minded people get to the top as a result of doing what they love.

5. **All great athletes are growth-minded.** They find success in learning and improving, not just winning.

6. **A leader with the "growth" mindset believes in the potential of employees, encourages teamwork, and has the courage to admit his mistakes.**

7. **In a romantic relationship, growth-minded people and couples work to help each other solve their problems and overcome their differences.** And when the relationship is over, they don't look for revenge; for them, it is all about understanding, forgiving, and moving on.

8. **Send a growth-mindset message to children that says: success depends on the efforts you invest in it, not on your innate abilities.** Praise your kids for their efforts and achievements they have made, teach them to set realistic goals, admit mistakes, and draw conclusions.

9. **If parents want to give their children a gift, the best thing they can do** is to teach their children to love challenges, be intrigued by mistakes, enjoy effort, and keep on learning.

10. **In order to master the "growth" mindset, you must accept that some "fixed" mindset dwells within you,** become aware of your fixed-mindset triggers and gradually develop new mental habits.

Mindset

Carol Dweck

Only people with a growth mindset can succeed and become outstanding leaders. A fixed-minded person is more likely to develop issues.

TWO MINDSETS

FIXED MINDSET

People with a "fixed" mindset believe that abilities are innate and stay the same during their lifetime.

GROWTH MINDSET

People with a "growth" mindset believe that innate abilities can and should be developed by investing effort.

Learning
- Fixed: As long as you have a talent or aptitudes, you don't need to invest effort in their development.
- Growth: Growth-minded people strive to develop their abilities, improve their skills and come up with new solutions.

Failures
- Fixed: Fixed-minded people don't try to learn from and repair their failures, they try to repair their self-esteem by looking for people who are even worse than they are.
- Growth: Addressing obstacles and setbacks head-on is the next step for learning.

Responsibility
- Fixed: People with the fixed mindset cannot accept responsibility for their failures, they assign blame or make excuses.
- Growth: If they are behind, they'll work harder, gain new experience, seek help, and try to catch up.

Success
- Fixed: Success is about establishing your superiority. If your talent does not get you to the top, then adverse circumstances are to blame.
- Growth: They enjoy the process of pursuing success and give it 100 percent, acquiring and sharpening their skills.

Outcome
- **Fixed-minded people achieve illusory success,** surround themselves with flatterers who extol their virtues, and hide from problems, blaming others every time they fail.
- **Growth-minded people achieve true success.** Believing that they can improve, they look squarely at their own mistakes and move forward with confidence and based on facts.

THE JOURNEY TO THE GROWTH MINDSET

STEP 1 — Embrace your fixed mindset

STEP 2 — Become aware of your fixed-mindset triggers

STEP 3 — Have a dialogue with your fixed mindset, educate it the essence of the growth mindset and observe how it makes you think

STATUS QUO: An internal monologue is **focused on judging**: "This means I'm a loser."

SHOULD BE: An internal monologue is **focused on constructive action**: "What can I learn from this?"

Personal development: 50 bestsellers in infographics

Letting Go: The Pathway of Surrender

David Hawkins

1. **We fear our inner feelings, because we fear we will be overwhelmed by them.** When we are afraid to face them, they continue to accumulate and become part of our subconscious, which makes them difficult to identify, and even more destructive and uncontrollable.

2. **Habitual mechanisms of protection from negative emotions** (suppression, displacement, expression, escape) do not allow us to use energy from these emotions in a constructive way.

3. **The acceptance and release of suppressed emotions** is a simple and efficient practice that reduces stress and cures many illnesses.

4. **Letting go and surrendering a feeling involves being aware of it, letting it surface, staying with it, and letting it run its course without wanting to alter it or do anything about it.** Essentially it means remaining an observer.

5. **Shame and fear are at the bottom of the scale of emotions, and love and peace are at the top.**

6. **It takes courage to stop being afraid and ashamed of your emotions and start developing awareness.** Courage is the critical point at which the shift from positive to negative energy takes place.

7. **By letting go of negativity, we release an enormous amount of energy.** It can easily be converted into love for healing us and the people around us.

8. **By letting go of negative feelings and emotions one by one,** we move up the scale of emotions, improving our quality of life.

9. **The ability to identify and understand your feelings (not thoughts) is important** for developing awareness and moving up the scale of emotions.

10. **It is advisable that you begin by merely observing your emotions and feelings.** This way, you'll be able to understand the relationship between feeling and thought. Finally, you learn to work with your feelings by acknowledging their existence and, without resisting or condemning them, you then begin to free up the energy stored in them.

Letting Go

David Hawkins

Letting go involves being aware of a feeling, letting it emerge, staying with it, and letting it run its course without wanting to make it different or do anything about it.

THE SCALE OF EMOTIONS

By letting go of negative feelings and emotions one by one, we move up the scale of emotions, improving our quality of life.

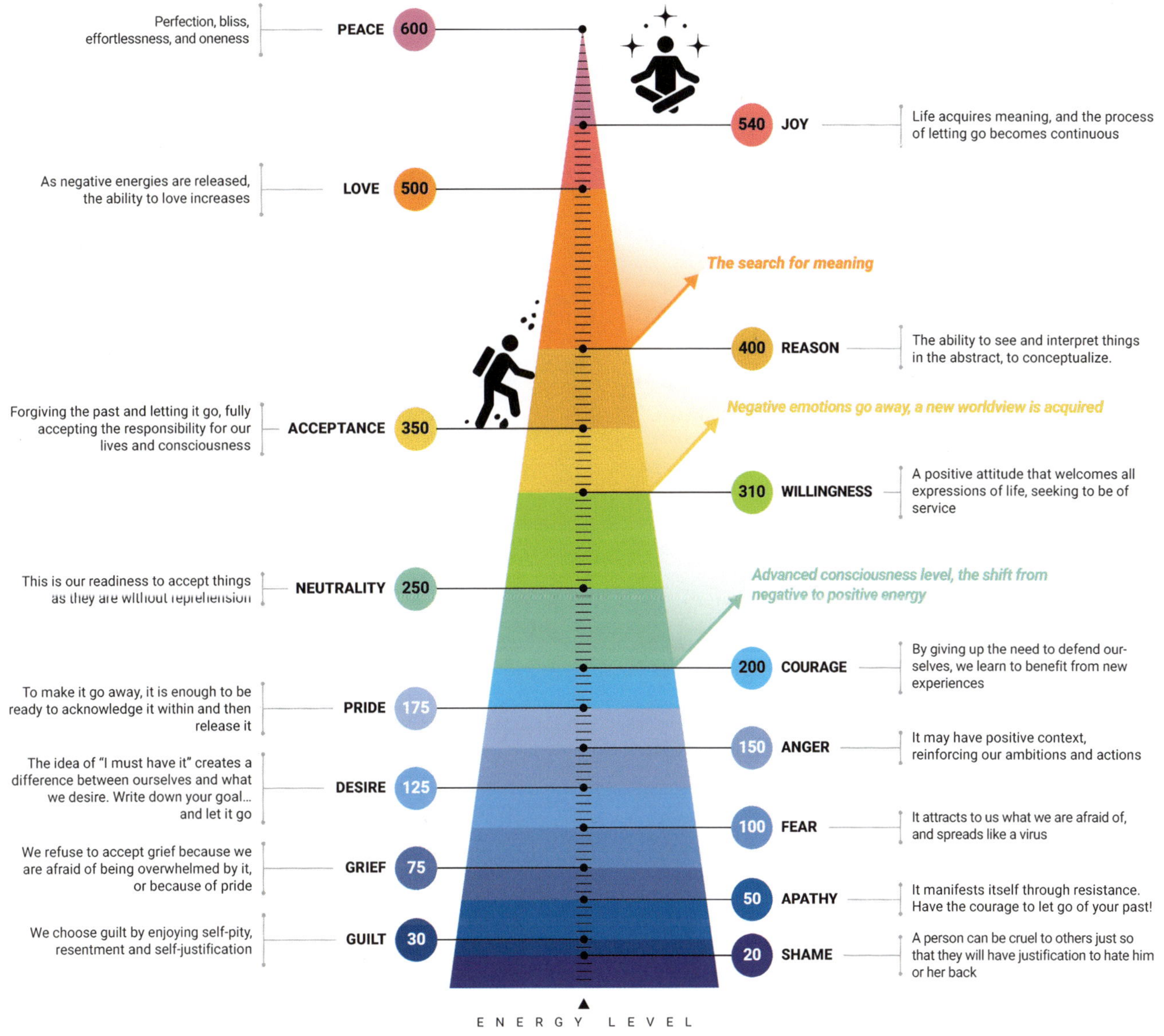

PEACE — 600 — Perfection, bliss, effortlessness, and oneness

JOY — 540 — Life acquires meaning, and the process of letting go becomes continuous

LOVE — 500 — As negative energies are released, the ability to love increases

The search for meaning

REASON — 400 — The ability to see and interpret things in the abstract, to conceptualize.

ACCEPTANCE — 350 — Forgiving the past and letting it go, fully accepting the responsibility for our lives and consciousness

Negative emotions go away, a new worldview is acquired

WILLINGNESS — 310 — A positive attitude that welcomes all expressions of life, seeking to be of service

NEUTRALITY — 250 — This is our readiness to accept things as they are without reprehension

Advanced consciousness level, the shift from negative to positive energy

COURAGE — 200 — By giving up the need to defend ourselves, we learn to benefit from new experiences

PRIDE — 175 — To make it go away, it is enough to be ready to acknowledge it within and then release it

ANGER — 150 — It may have positive context, reinforcing our ambitions and actions

DESIRE — 125 — The idea of "I must have it" creates a difference between ourselves and what we desire. Write down your goal... and let it go

FEAR — 100 — It attracts to us what we are afraid of, and spreads like a virus

GRIEF — 75 — We refuse to accept grief because we are afraid of being overwhelmed by it, or because of pride

APATHY — 50 — It manifests itself through resistance. Have the courage to let go of your past!

GUILT — 30 — We choose guilt by enjoying self-pity, resentment and self-justification

SHAME — 20 — A person can be cruel to others just so that they will have justification to hate him or her back

ENERGY LEVEL

THREE STAGES OF UNDERSTANDING EMOTIONS

1 OBSERVATION — Learning to identify your feelings and emotions, observing the relationship between an emerging thought and emotion

2 EXPERIMENTATION — Setting aside certain aspects of your recurring thoughts and indentifying the feelings and emotions associated with them

3 LIVING THROUGH — Not just accepting that a feeling exists, but letting it be until it runs out

Thanks for the Feedback: The Science and Art of Receiving Feedback Well

Douglas Stone, Sheila Heen

1. **We live in a world of feedback.** Receiving feedback, just like giving it, is a tough challenge.

2. **Feedback is beneficial.** The people who do not shy away from feedback are better performers. Even when feedback is unfair, it helps us become better. It's up to us whether we can make good use of feedback.

3. **Feedback is stressful.** But if we learn to accept in in the right way, it helps us feel comfortable and confident.

4. **You need to learn to identify and overcome your natural resistance to feedback.** Ask questions and gain useful information from any feedback, no matter how unfair it may seem.

5. **Feedback may include three types of messages: appreciation, coaching, or evaluation.** Learn to separate them in order to understand what your communication partner wants and what benefit you can get out of it.

6. **There are three types of triggers that prevent us from accepting feedback constructively:** truth triggers, relationship triggers, and identity triggers.

7. **Truth triggers say, "This feedback is unfair".** In order to remove these triggers, separate appreciation from coaching and evaluation and request the kind of feedback that you need. It is important that you not mix up the different feedback types when you comment on other people's actions.

8. **Relationship triggers are set off when we mistrust the feedback giver and question his or her motivation.** In order to address these triggers, don't expect to be loved. Remember that being a bystander allows you to focus on the content of the feedback, not the form of delivery.

9. **Identity triggers are set off when feedback questions your relationship with yourself.** Separate your emotions, your interpretations and the actual feedback you get. Cultivate a growth identity. Give up the belief that you are perfect and see feedback as something that helps you improve.

10. **You can and should turn down negative feedback.** Draw a boundary when feedback givers attack your character, not your behavior, make threats, when it is always you who has to change, or when they set impossible challenges.

Thanks for the Feedback

Douglas Stone, Sheila Heen

The people who do not shy away from feedback are better and they get more enjoyment from doing their job, while the inability to accept criticism creates conflicts and tensions.

THREE TRIGGERS THAT BLOCK FEEDBACK

TRUTH TRIGGERS
Are set off when feedback is perceived as unfair
("**This is plain wrong!**")

RELATIONSHIP TRIGGERS
Are set off when we mistrust the feedback giver
("**They've got no credibility on this topic!**")

IDENTITY TRIGGERS
Are set off when feedback threatens who you are ("**Well, of course, I always spoil everything!**")

MANAGING OUR REACTIONS

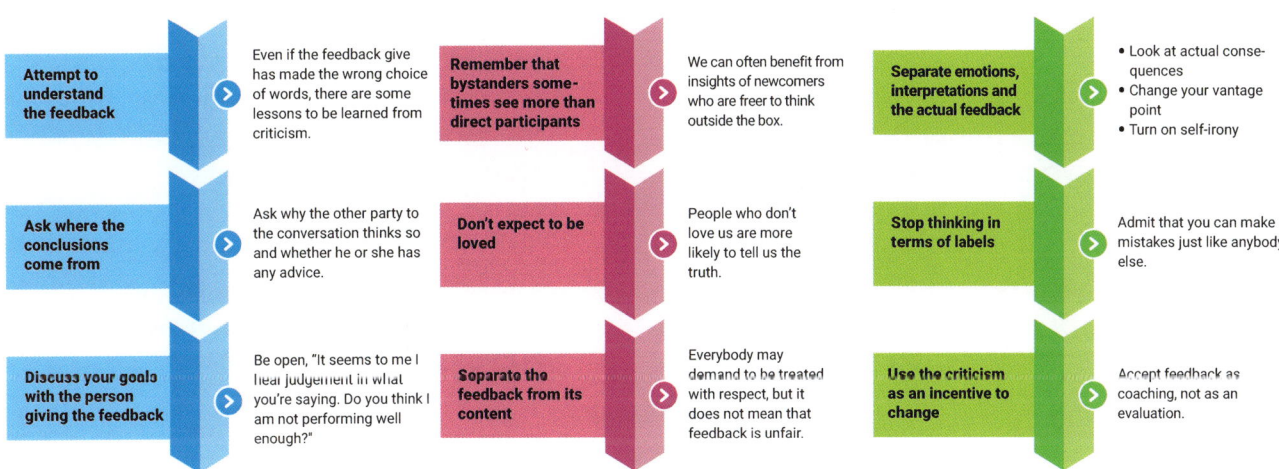

FEEDBACK IN CONVERSATION

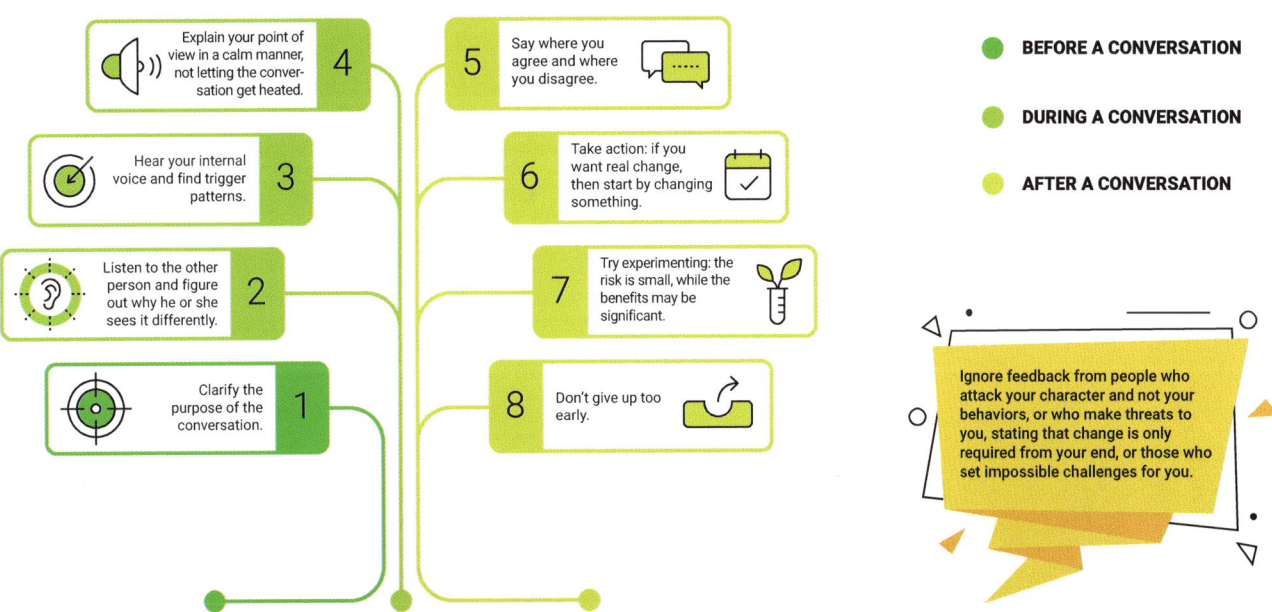

- **BEFORE A CONVERSATION**
- **DURING A CONVERSATION**
- **AFTER A CONVERSATION**

Ignore feedback from people who attack your character and not your behaviors, or who make threats to you, stating that change is only required from your end, or those who set impossible challenges for you.

Emergent Strategy: Shaping Change, Changing Worlds

Adrienne Brown

1. **Tiny creatures (fungi, dandelions, roaches, etc.)** continue to survive and grow through fusion, not competition, while the "kings" of the jungle (lions, tigers, bears) are going extinct.

2. **If we stop competing and organize ourselves as a community,** we as a species will avoid extinction and continue to thrive.

3. **The emergent strategy explains the rules for living in alignment with our home (universe)** and each other, and is about transforming ourselves in order to create and accept a world of justice and freedom.

4. **The emergent strategy is based on observations of the natural world and consists of six elements:** Fractality, Interdependence and Decentralization, Intentional Adaptation, Non-linearity and Iteration, Resilience and Transformative Justice, and Creating More Possibilities.

5. **Fractality means that how we behave in small scale is how we are in large scale.** In order to change the world, you must start with changing yourself.

6. **Interdependence and Decentralization mean that anyone can be a leader.** If you trust people, they will become trustworthy.

7. **Intentional Adaptation means that you need to go with the flow of change to stay in control.** Change will happen, therefore the intention we have when change happens is key.

8. **Non-linearity and Iteration tell you that life happens in cycles.** Sometimes one step is enough to break a vicious cycle and start doing right things.

9. **Resilience and Transformative Justice mean that the ability to recover from disasters is essential.** Every bad thing that happens teaches us a lesson.

10. **Creating More Possibilities means adapting your uniqueness so you can work in a team.** By applying the emergent strategy, we will help both ourselves and others.

Emergent Strategy

Adrienne Brown

The natural world holds the secrets to our continued existence, which mankind could apply to its world in order to both survive and flourish.

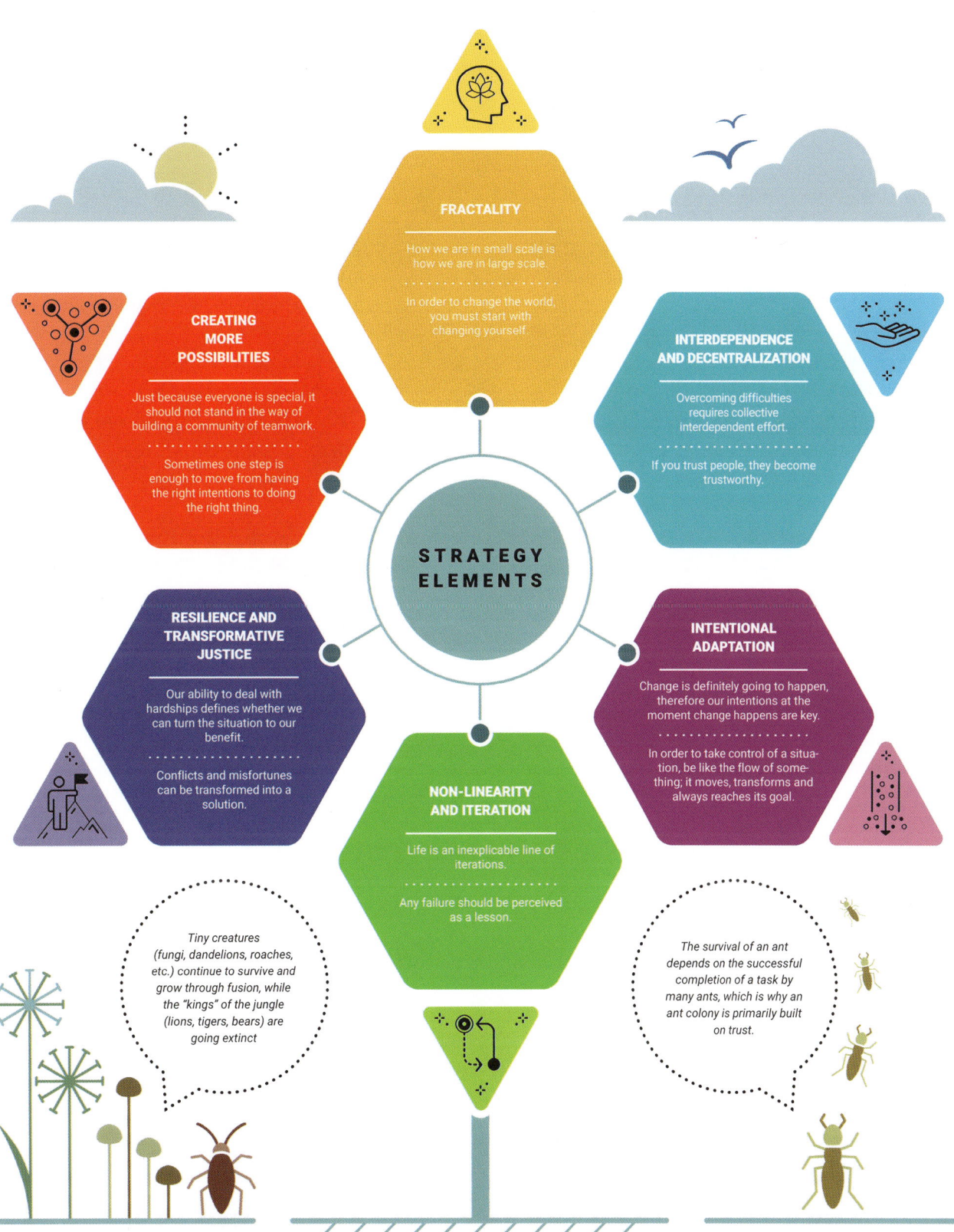

Everything is Negotiable! How to Get the Best Deal Every Time

Gavin Kennedy

1. **Negotiations are only successful if there is a zero-sum game.** Stay away from simple solutions, the desire to win at all costs, and a readiness to concede.

2. **There are four types of negotiators.** A Donkey is someone who is stubborn, will not listen to the other party, and rejects any compromise. A Sheep is timid, lacks confidence, and agrees to anything. A Sly Fox is a dodger, goal-oriented and unscrupulous. An Owl is a virtuoso in negotiations who is succeeds at reaching a compromise in an ethical manner.

3. **Every human has been involved in the negotiating process since his or her birth.** Babies give a stubborn "donkey" cry when they are hungry; a toddler grows to develop "slyness". Each of us is an experienced negotiator.

4. **The worst thing you can do with any negotiator is to accept his first offer.** He will think that he should have offered a higher price, and you will definitely find blemishes in what you negotiated for.

5. **There is no such thing as a fixed price.** When you set a price, it conveys your attitude toward the object of the sale. Don't give away your lack of confidence by adding "or best offer" after you price it.

6. **If you've been let down, don't complain and don't make accusations.** Take the initiative and suggest that you renegotiate. You will get what you desire and remove the emotional burden from both parties.

7. **Concessions are useless.** Goodwill concessions by one party don't "soften up" the other party, they make him or her tougher.

8. **If the pressure is too high, pretend that you cannot make a decision without the real "decision-maker" (if there is no such person — invent one).**

9. **Be calm and firm in saying "no" to unacceptable demands.** But keep in mind that the most useful negotiating word is IF.

10. **Don't give in to insults, don't bend under pressure or threats,** don't pay attention to corporate trappings or glitter and always have in mind some workarounds (such as alternative suppliers, plan B's, etc.).

Everything is Negotiable!

Gavin Kennedy

Gavin Kennedy's book is a tutorial on negotiating not only in business, but in other fields of life. It will help you learn more about the negotiating process and make it more efficient.

NEGOTIATOR TYPES

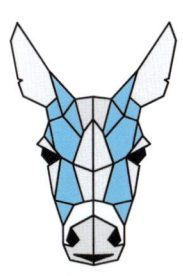

DONKEY — Stubborn and predictable
Never agrees to a compromise. Unable to calculate two-three moves in advance

SHEEP — Compliant, obedient and easily intimidated
Makes all kinds of concessions, agrees to any offers

SLY FOX — Cunning and shifty
Has a clear vision of what he wants and is convinced that he will get it. Does not care too much about moral standards

OWL — Wise and intelligent
The guru of the negotiating process. Follows ethical standards: does not take advantage of the counter-party and treats his him or her with respect.

NEGOTIATIONS ARE ONLY SUCCESSFUL IF THERE IS NO LOSING PARTY!

NEGOTIATING RULES

NEGOTIATORS EXPECT TO NEGOTIATE
The worst thing you can do to a negotiator is to accept the first offer he or she makes. Don't accept it even if it is "an offer you can't refuse."

DON'T COMPLAIN
Trying to negotiate a remedy is much more constructive than complaining. When you are the one who proposes a remedy, you are taking into account your own interests.

MANDATE TACTICS
In order to cool off an aggressive negotiator, it is important to build a negotiating platform by claiming that some principal who isn't present has allegedly determined the terms you must stick to in the negotiations.

DON'T ADD "OR BEST OFFER"
A potential buyer sees that the seller is afraid of not selling his or her product. When you set a price, it reflects your vision of how much a product, or a service is worth.

DON'T MAKE CONCESSIONS
Resist the temptation to concede the part of the deal that you regard as valuable. If you have conceded once, you will be expected to make more concessions.

MAGIC WORDS "NO" AND "IF"
When you respond with "no," it makes your positions tougher in the eyes of the other party, and saying "if" helps break a deadlock, such as: "If you agree to drop 20% off the price, I will immediately place an offer."

TIPS TO INFLUENCE THE COURSE OF NEGOTIATIONS

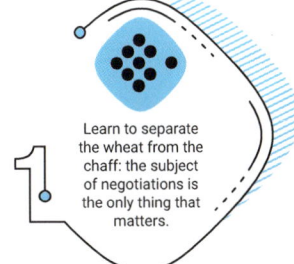
1. Learn to separate the wheat from the chaff: the subject of negotiations is the only thing that matters.

2. Insults and impudence are bad negotiating tactics. Don't let such tactics lead you astray.

3. Insightful negotiators do not resort to open pressure or threats.

4. Out-in-the-open expensive props do not necessarily reflect the true power of the one who uses them.

A Complaint is a Gift: Using Customer Feedback As a Strategic Tool

Janelle Barlow, Klaus Moeller

1 **Clients are always entitled to dissatisfaction,** even if we consider their complaints absurd, unfounded or improper.

2 **By making a complaint, customers show that they still trust the company and offer it an opportunity to fix the situation.** The least loyal clients don't spend their time on complaints.

3 **A fundamental change in attitude is required if businesses want to retain complaining customers.** They need to learn to put themselves in the disappointed people's shoes and realize the value of a complaint for achieving their business goals.

4 **Complaints are a crucial source of valuable information that cannot be obtained anywhere else.** Complaint handlers should focus on the content of a complaint, not its form.

5 **Collected statistics suggest that if customers** believe their complaints are welcomed and responded to, they will more likely repurchase.

6 **An ineffective complaint policy can start a negative chain reaction:** customers leave a business dissatisfied, the public begins to identify the business as a place where it does no good to complain, customers stop complaining, product and service quality are therefore not improved, staff feel less motivated, which, in turn, leads to more customers leaving the business dissatisfied.

7 **Customers want different responses depending on what happened to them.** One useful way to figure that out is to sort complaints into two groups: **1)** complaints about issues that can be fixed; **2)** complaints about situations that cannot be fixed, but about which customers nevertheless want to be heard and have their feelings acknowledged.

8 **In order to convert a dissatisfied customer into a loyal one, companies can respond to a complaint by offering:** a sincere apology, a price reduction, a free product or gift, a coupon for future price reductions, and/or an assurance that something has been changed inside the organization to prevent this from happening again.

9 **Before you apologize, thank the client for communicating valuable information.** Correct the mistake, offer compensation, and make sure that your customer remains satisfied.

10 **Punish your processes, not your people.** Make sure customer complaints continue to be treated as a gift in your organization.

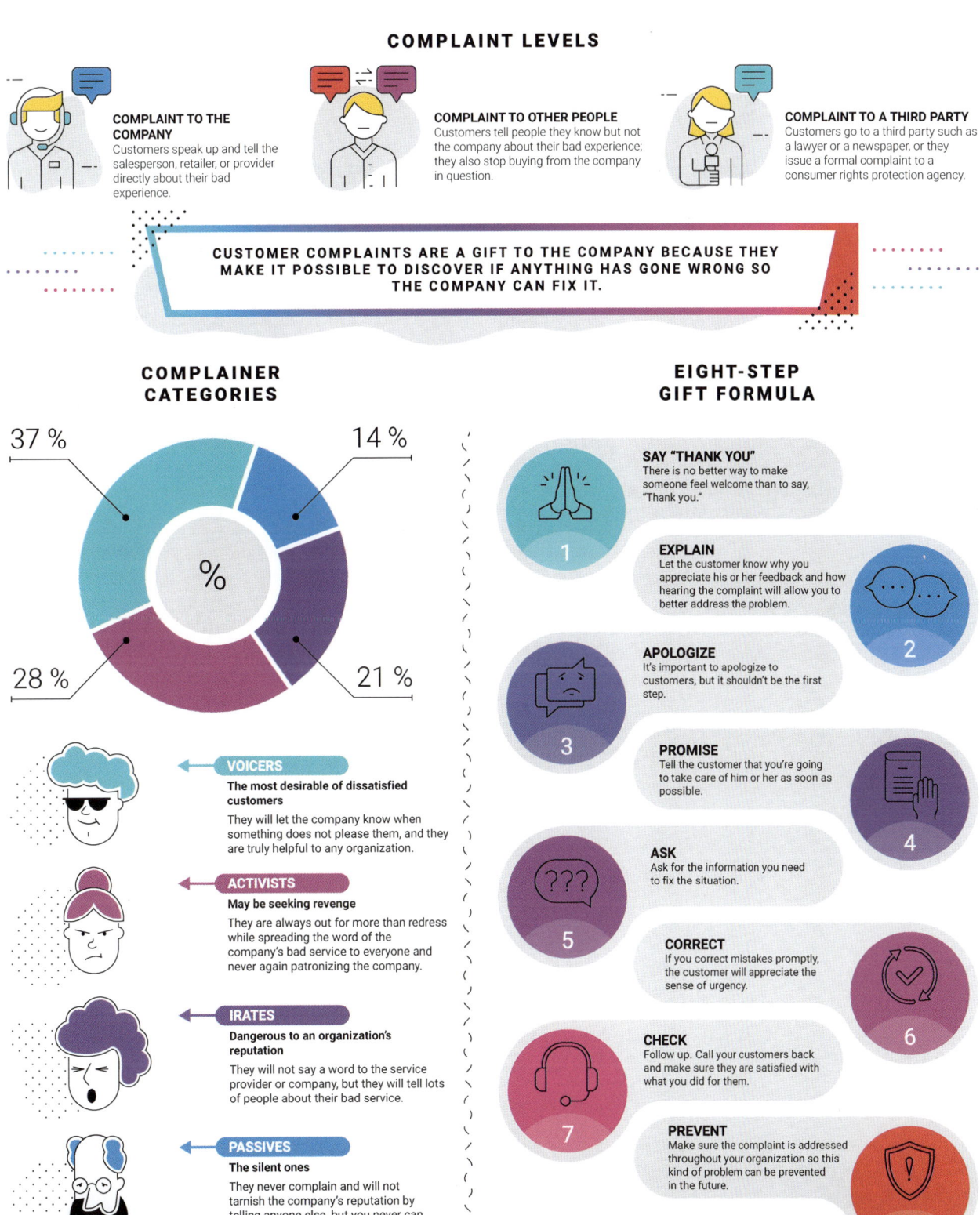

Influencer: The Power to Change Anything

Kerry Patterson, Joseph Grenny, David Maxfield, Ron McMillan, Al Switzler

1. **When we discover** we cannot affect change we surrender.

2. **Influencers always strive to do better** and can identify vital behaviors in order to influence them.

3. **Use the experience of successful influencers** with tried-and-tested tactics.

4. **Look for positive deviance** in order to reproduce your own or somebody else's successful experience in the future.

5. **Influence others vicariously through someone else or a story.**

6. **Since our ineffectiveness at influencing others stems from a lack of motivation,** the solution lies in continued learning.

7. **When working with a team,** if you partner with the opinion leader so that other team members get behind him, they get behind you.

8. **When you face a difficult task,** make others part of the solution.

9. **Use structural motivation only after you have successfully applied personal and social motivation.**

10. **Don't ignore items around you —** sometimes using them is enough to influence human behavior.

Influencer

Kerry Patterson, Joseph Grenny, David Maxfield, Ron McMillan, Al Switzler

The secret to becoming a successful influencer lies in your continuously striving to do better and having the ability to find a key to people's hearts.

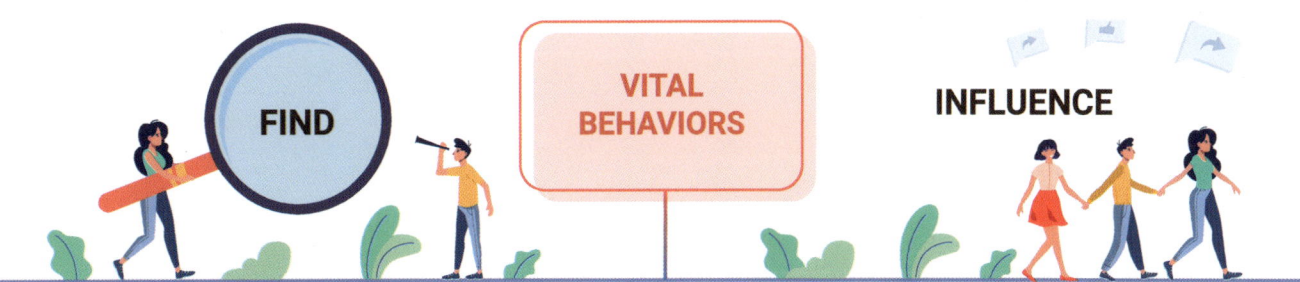

Focus on vital behaviors
If you change vital behaviors, problems topple like a house of cards.

Look for positive deviance
Copy your own or somebody else's successful experience.

Study the best
Many tactics have been tried and tested in practice.

Create a vicarious experience
When you expose subjects to other people who are demonstrating a vital behavior, the subjects learn from the surrogate's successes and failures.

Apply immersive techniques
Tell people stories that can fully captivate your listeners.

» SIX SOURCES OF INFLUENCE «

MOTIVATION — Virtually all forces that affect human behavior work in two domains: motivation or ability. — **ABILITY**

PERSONAL

Motivation:
- Connect to a person's sense of self
- Connect the person's behavior to his or her moral values
- Win hearts by talking to people about what they want

Ability:
- Demand your own full attention for brief intervals
- Provide immediate feedback against a clear standard
- Break mastery into mini-goals, don't focus on long-term goals
- Interpret setbacks as guides, not brakes

SOCIAL

Motivation:
- Find opinion leaders and influence them

Ability:
- When you face a difficult task, make others part of the problem

STRUCTURAL

Motivation:
- Reward little behaviors, not just results
- Don't engage in rewarding others if other tactics proved successful
- Avoid rewarding the wrong behaviors
- Although punishment should be avoided, it is sometimes necessary
- Make sure that fair warning is given before punishment

Ability:
- Take action against spatial incompetence:
  - Make invisible things visible
  - If staff don't cooperate, position their desks next to each other
  - Pay attention to the office environment

Personal development: 50 bestsellers in infographics

The Leader Who Had No Title: A Modern Fable on Real Success in Business and in Life

Robin Sharma

1. **It is up to everyone to choose whether he or she wants to be a leader or a victim, to suffer or to be happy, to accept or to reject responsibility.**

2. **There is an inner leader in everyone of us, but not everyone uses his or her leadership potential.** We are waiting for a special moment or global changes, but in most cases, it never comes. And we only have ourselves to blame.

3. **You don't need a title or positive opinions of others to be a leader.** You need only be passionately committed to your vision and have the strength to carry out positive transformations.

4. **Unlike victims, leaders love a challenge, as it makes growth more exciting.** The organizations that cultivate leadership without titles gain enormous advantages in difficult times.

5. **People do not dare to leave their safety zone, because they start feeling "weird" and become afraid of making mistakes.** However, any time you try something new it is going to feel weird, while fear is a dead-end street.

6. **Master communication skills and learn to value people, as it is essential for your career and for having a rich life.**

7. **Business is about being helpful.** When you are honestly helping others, they try to help you.

8. **Before you become a leader for others, you need to become a leader for yourself.** In order to gain inner power, grow your internal life and get rid of limiting beliefs regarding your leadership potential.

9. **Use the four natural leadership powers that live in everyone:** the power to express the absolute best within yourself, the power to inspire, the power to drive positive change in the face of negative conditions, and the power to treat all stakeholders with respect, appreciation and kindness — to raise the organization's culture to best of breed.

10. **Exercise your body and your mind, keep an eye on what you eat and what you think,** practice affirmations and visualization, journalize, and never stop learning — these are the fundamentals of leadership without a title.

The Leader Who Had No Title

Robin Sharma

Personal development: 50 bestsellers in infographics

The Innovator's DNA: Mastering the Five Skills of Disruptive Innovators

Jeff Dyer, Hal Gregersen, Clayton Christensen

1. **Only a third of our ability to think creatively depends on genetics** — this means creativity can be developed.

2. **Innovators differ from regular people** in that they have innovative courage and possess five advanced discovery skills.

3. **The first skill, Associating,** is a cognitive skill that is central to an innovator's DNA.

4. **Associating is the ability to successfully connect seemingly unrelated questions, problems, or ideas from completely different fields.**

5. **The four other skills are behavioral.** They are questioning, observing, experimenting, and networking.

6. **Developing discovery skills requires that people consider their priorities,** evaluate their discovery skills, identify the motivating factor for developing those skills, work hard on them, and then find the right mentor.

7. **If you want your children to grow up to be creative adults,** start developing their discovery skills as soon as possible.

8. **Innovative organizations are usually led by innovators,** but apart from their creative leaders, these organizations have DNA that consists of a 3P frame-work: people, processes, and philosophies.

9. **Innovative courage implies striving to shatter stereotypes and being ready to take smart risks.**

10. **Discovery processes in an organization are successful if innovation is everyone's jobjob.** Innovation project teams should be small and properly organized, and the people in them should be ready to take risks.

The Innovator's DNA

Jeff Dyer, Hal Gregersen, Clayton Christensen

Innovators come up with groundbreaking new ideas not only due to the power of their mind, but also as a result of their behavior. By changing your behavior, you can improve your creativity.

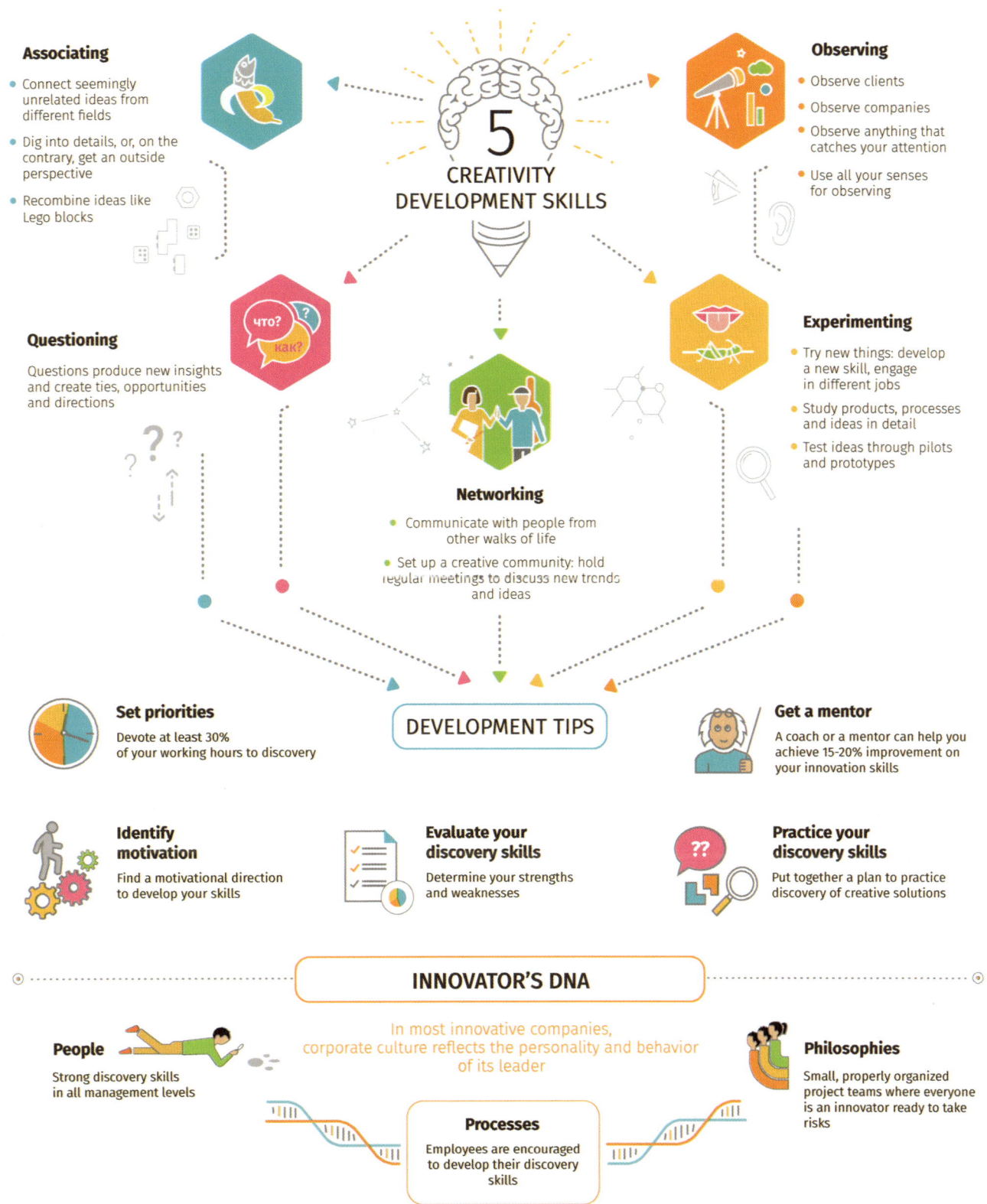

Tribal Leadership: Leveraging Natural Groups to Build a Thriving Organization

Dave Logan, John King, Halee Fischer-Wright

1. **People live in tribes: like in the ice age, every person's tribe consists of 20 to 150 people.** You may be in more than one tribe: at your workplace, among the parents of your kids' classmates, at church, or on social networks.

2. **Every corporate tribe has a dominant culture, which we can rate on a scale of a one to five, with five being the most desirable.** These stages have a direct impact on a company's success regardless of the race, gender, education or living standards of the people in the tribe.

3. **Each time people speak, their words exhibit the characteristics of one of five tribal stages.** When a people learn the language of a higher stage, their behavior and mindset change, and they move up a stage.

4. **People and groups move up only one stage at a time.** However, they can crash down very quickly.

5. **True leaders are the people who understand the language of each stage and are good at influencing people at different stages.**

6. **People at stage one are extremely hostile.** In order get to the next stage, people must see that others live differently, be willing to change, cut ties with people at their current stage, and get to know people at higher stages.

7. **People at stage two disconnect themselves from organizational concerns and do the minimum to get by, all while hiding their laziness from their boss.** Those who want tto climb up a stage must shoot for success, establish relationships with people at stage three, and start discussing their work with colleagues in one-on-one sessions.

8. **Stage three is the dominant culture among about 50% of workplace tribes.** These people are "lone warriors", they don't like to help, but they enjoy gossiping. They can move up by starting to share information and working in partnership, but only after forgoing egocentricity and manipulative behavior.

9. **At stage four, teams are the normare the norm.** They are focused on shared values and a common purpose. Information moves freely throughout the group. Transition to stage five is possible when people are focused on their business, accept no obstacles in the pursuit of their goal, and don't compete with anybody.

10. **Stage five is the future of the business.** People in this culture can find a way to work with almost anyone provided that their commitment to company values has the same level of intensity as their own.

Tribal Leadership

Dave Logan, John King, Halee Fischer-Wright

The tribal leader focuses primarily on building up the tribe or, more precisely, upgrading the tribe's culture. If the leader is successful, tribal members recognize him or her as their leader and put forth their best effort. The higher a corporate culture stage is, the more efficiently the tribe performs.

HOW TO BECOME A TRIBAL LEADER?

- Learn the language and customs of all five cultural stages
- Understand which tribal members speak which language – in essence, who is at what stage?
- Build a support network around you so that you are stable at Stage Four
- Be in contact with people at Stage Four and Five

90 days to assend to the next level

5 — INNOCENT WONDERMENT
LIFE IS GREAT
- People embody the company's values
- Potential is bounded only by imagination and group commitment
- No fear, stress or workplace conflicts
- Successful cooperation among people and companies with different values
- Developed infrastructure is in place

AFTER A WHILE STAGE FIVE GROUPS RECEDE TO STAGE FOUR

STAGE FIVE TRIBES ARE THE FUTURE OF THE BUSINESS

4 — TRIBAL PRIDE
WE'RE THE BEST
- Focus on a common purpose
- Information moves freely
- Shared values
- Partnerships are formed to accomplish what's important at the moment
- Team spirit

- Encourage them to form triads
- Discuss and implement a tribe strategy together (values, goals, performance, assets, actions)
- Encourage them to aim high (not only win, but to make history)
- Create optimal conditions for development

3 — LONE WARRIOR
I'M THE BEST
- Personal interest
- Resistance to sharing information
- Rumors and gossips
- Ambitions
- Arrogance
- Complaints about lack of support

- Encourage them to work on projects that are bigger than anything they can do alone
- Inspire them by example
- Teach them that real power comes not from knowledge but from networks
- Describe role models that are exhibiting stage-four behavior

2 — APATHETIC VICTIM
MY LIFE SUCKS
- No initiative or passion
- Doing the minimum to get by
- Hostility to changes
- Unwillingness to develop
- Lack of interpersonal communication

- Inspire and support
- Encourage them to establish dyadic relationships
- Encourage them to establish relationships with people at higher stages

1 — DESPERATE HOSTILITY
LIFE SUCKS
- Alienated from organizational concerns
- Lack of morality
- Every man for himself

- Lead them to a community of a higher stage
- Help them cut ties with people of stage one
- Inspire them with examples of positive change

Personal development: 50 bestsellers in infographics

Good to Great: Why Some Companies Make the Leap… and Others Don't

Jim Collins

1. **For great companies, money is not the end but the means.**

2. **Great companies always have talented leaders.**

3. **The best leaders accept responsibility for their failures and don't boast about their achievements.** They value company success over their own well-being.

4. **Leaders of great companies don't try to improve the discipline and motivation of their personnel.** They only hire disciplined and motivated people.

5. **A company can become great at the intersection of three key dimensions:** its people do what they're passionate about; they do what they can be the best in the world at; management uses an economic model that earns money.

6. **Technologies can help a company accelerate its growth,** but they don't make it a great company.

7. **Great companies appear boring and pedestrian-looking from the outside,** but upon closer inspection, they're full of people who display extreme diligence and stunning intensity.

8. **There is always a buildup before a breakthrough;** if you jump right into a breakthrough, you're in the loop of doom.

9. **Leaders of great companies lead with questions, not answers;** they engage in dialogue and debate, not coercion; they address mistakes, not assign blame.

10. **Great companies regard the right people as their most important asset.**

Good to Great

Jim Collins

Jim Collins wrote this book as a major and detailed study. He explored dozens of successful companies, and hundreds of managers, looking for crumbs of knowledge about ways to develop a great business and become a successful leader.

 Creates superb results and demonstrates a compelling personal humility

 More of a hedgehog than a fox. A hedgehog focuses on a single competence where his company can be the best in the world

 Looks out the window to apportion credit for the success of the company; looks in the mirror to apportion responsibility for poor results

A GREAT MANAGER
Channels his or her ambition into the company!

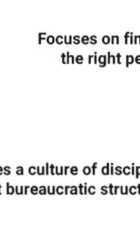 Focuses on finding the right people

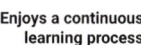 Creates a culture of discipline, not bureaucratic structures

 Enjoys a continuous learning process

GET THE RIGHT PEOPLE ON THE JOB
- Hires talented, responsible and dedicated professionals who are passionate about what they do
- Self-disciplined people don't need to be managed; they follow a consistent system with clear constraints

DEFINE YOUR STRATEGY
- What you can be the best in the world at
- What drives your economic engine
- What are you deeply passionate about

ELIMINATE CLASS DISTINCTIONS
- Create an egalitarian meritocracy that makes sure there are no demotivating factors for people

CREATE A CLIMATE WHERE THE TRUTH IS HEARD
- Lead with questions, not answers
- Engage in dialogue and debate
- Conduct autopsies, without blame
- Build red flag mechanisms that turn simple information into information that cannot be ignored

MAKE GOOD USE OF TECHNOLOGIES
- Apply carefully selected pioneering technologies. Introduce them in a thoughtful and inventive manner

MAINTAIN SUSTAINABLE TRANSFORMATION
- Disregard things that you can just do well, focus on what you can be the best in the world at

Principles: Life and Work

Ray Dalio

1. **Be realistic, but never lose the ability to dream.** Be honest to yourself about your dreams, and don't give up on them due to fear.

2. **Your principles have to reflect values you really believe in.** By questioning all pre-packaged principles, you will be able to find the one you believe works best.

3. **Develop your self-reflection abilities and be as honest as possible with yourself and the people around you.** Everyone has weaknesses, but one of the most important things that differentiate successful people is that they are aware of their weaknesses and figure out how to work around them.

4. **When you hire people, pay more attention to their life values and abilities than to their experience.** You will only be able to put together a strong business team if their values are aligned with yours.

5. **When you evaluate your people, make sure they aren't more concerned with looking good than about achieving their goals;** see whether they accept responsibility, whether they are able to get over discomfort and make the most of the process of encountering reality, whether they are able to make decisions that are based on more than short-term benefits.

6. **Watch out for the unfocused and unproductive "we should (do something)."** It's important to identify the people who are responsible for the result by their names. Assign responsibilities based on people's abilities, not job titles.

7. **Understand the difference between managing, micromanaging and not managing.** Managing primarily means constantly improving business processes.

8. **Learn to distribute your time between doing routine tasks and moving towards your strategic tasks.** It is important not to confuse "goals" and "desires".

9. **Don't give up if you run across problems.** Most of the problems are merely development-stage growing pains. By getting past them, you are getting closer to what you want out of life.

10. **If you don't evolve, you are slowly dying.** Be open to new knowledge and new views of life, and don't be afraid to shoot for ambitious goals.

Principles: Life and Work

Ray Dalio

Knowing and sticking to his principles helped Ray Dalio build Bridgewater, an investment company with over $160 billion in assets.

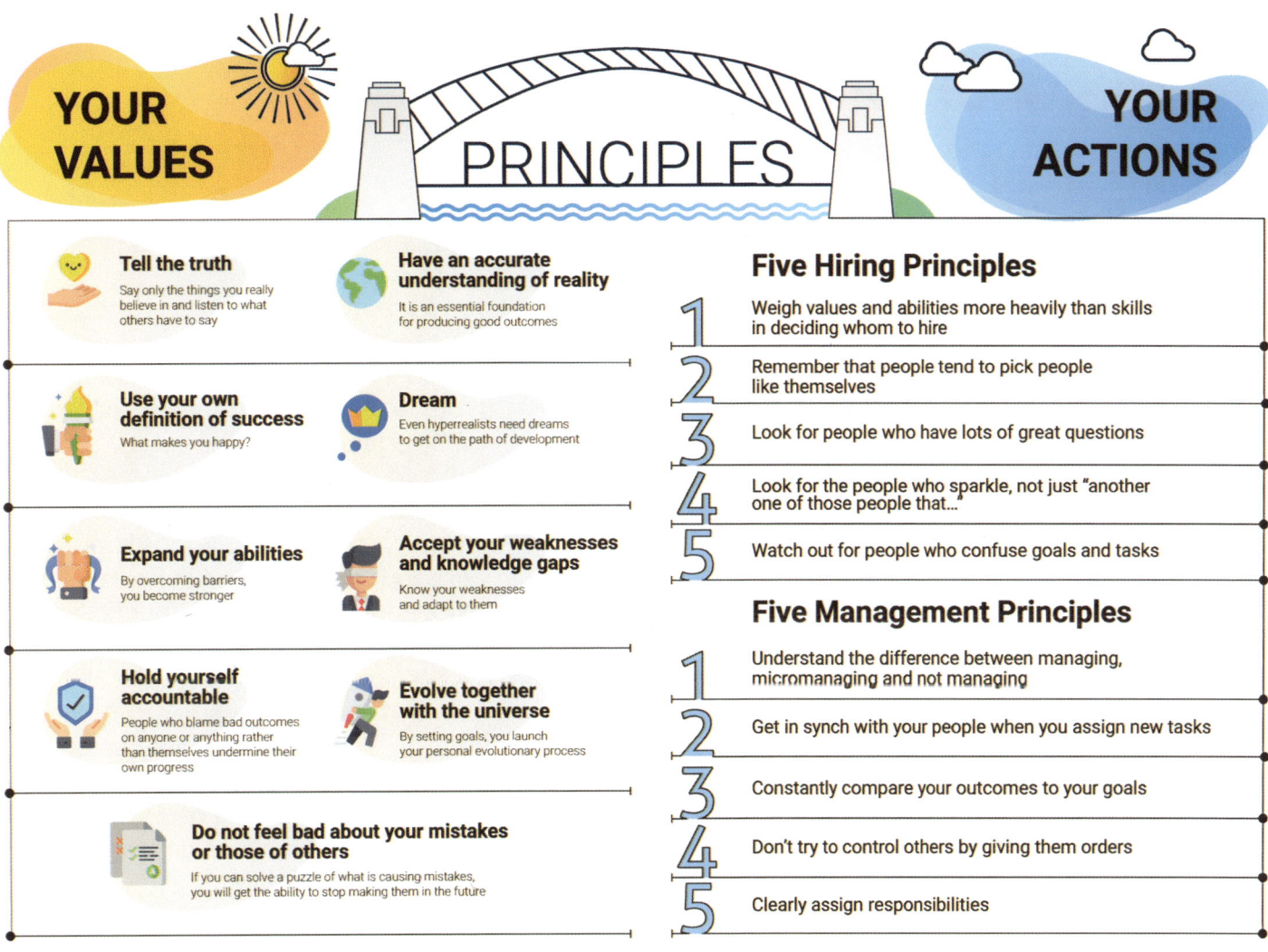

Personal development: 50 bestsellers in infographics

Leading The Leaders: How To Enrich Your Style of Management and Handle People Whose Style Is Different From Yours

Ichak Adizes

1. **The four roles of management (PAEI): the Producer (P), the Administrator (A), the Entrepreneur (E) and the Integrator (I) — cannot be performed with excellence by the same person.**

2. **Good management is only possible when different roles are handled by different people.** The solution is to put together a team.

3. **A management team requires people with different mindsets and management styles that can complement, rather that clone each other.**

4. **The purpose of managerial education should not be to create ideal (PAEI) managers, but to train normal human beings to accept their deficiencies and learn how to work with others who complement their strengths and weaknesses.**

5. **Effective leaders of a complementary team must be aware of what they are doing and understand the consequences and meaning of their actions, including the impact their behavior has on other people's behavior.** They can identify excellence and weaknesses in others, as well as accept and appreciate differences in others, and hire and develop people who are different from them.

6. **You can be a good manager without (I) as long as you are strong in two or even three other roles — (PAei, PaEi, pAEi, PAEi).** but unless one of them is Integrator, you not be a leader.

7. **To be a leader means being able to lead.** To know how to lead your subordinates, your colleagues, and even your boss, you must know how to handle all four styles.

8. **If managers of four different styles look through a window, they see totally different things.** An Entrepreneur sees the big picture, an Administrator sees that the frame is dirty, a Producer is busy thinking about the window's functionality, while an Integrator is looking at the other guys and wondering, "What are you guys looking at?"

9. **Each management style has its own weaknesses.** A Producer is not good at delegating. An Administrator is not ready to take risks. An Entrepreneur switches back and forth from one idea to another and never brings any of them to completion. An Integrator has a problem with making tough decisions and is sensitive to what others may think.

10. **Misunderstandings are the main source of conflicts within an organization.** If you want to be understood, you have to be the one who adapts.

Leading The Leaders

Ichak Adizes

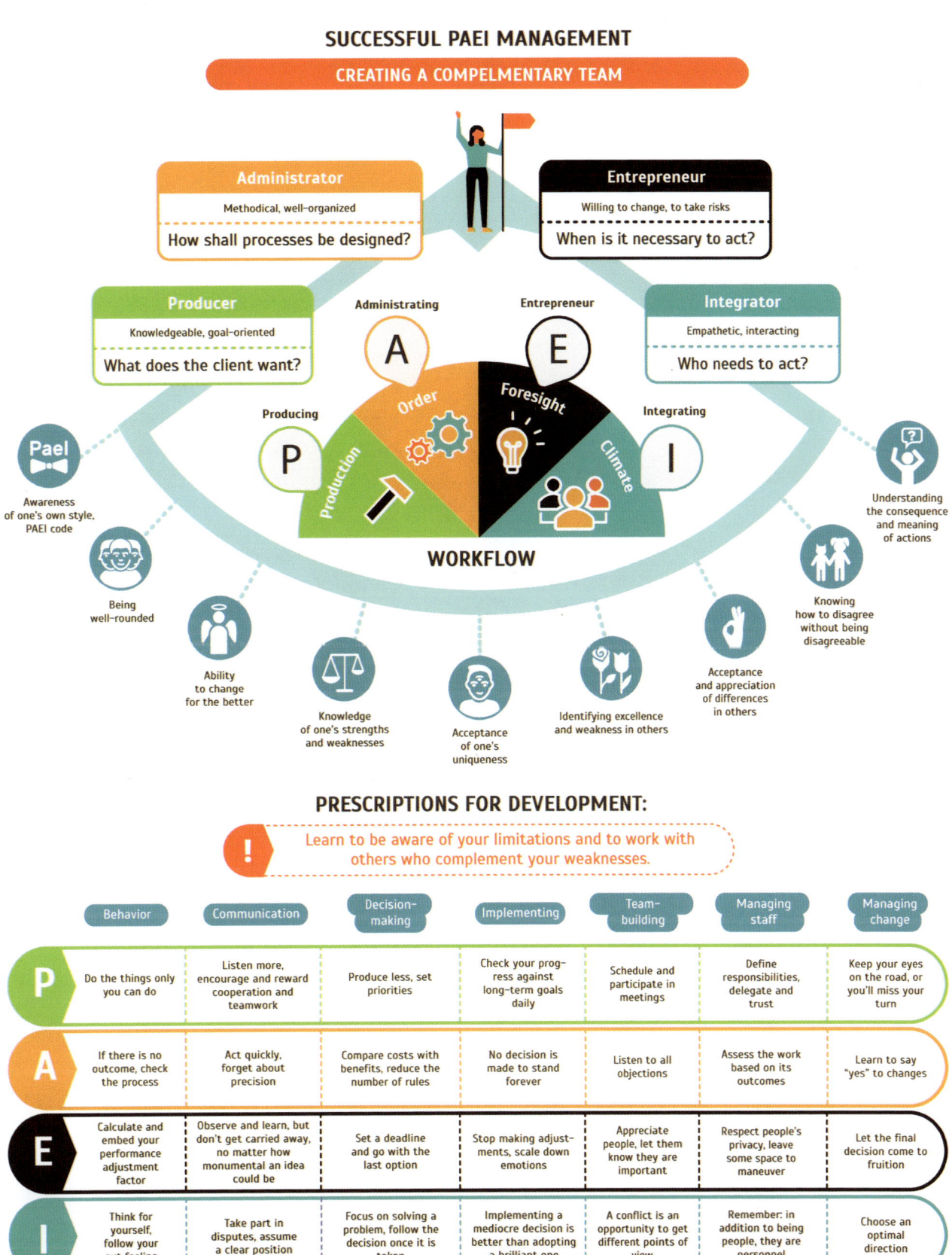

Personal development: 50 bestsellers in infographics

Great by Choice: Uncertainty, Chaos and Luck — Why Some Thrive Despite Them All

Jim Collins, Morten Hansen

1. **Leaders of companies that grew tenfold were not visionaries,** innovated on the same level as their competitors, and didn't always react to external change.

2. **Great companies do not generally have more luck than their competitors,** but they make the most of it.

3. **Getting the right people in leadership positions is the best luck a great company can have.**

4. **Problems and failures make great companies stronger,** because their leaders know how to benefit from a crisis.

5. **Tenfold leaders always possess three core behaviors both in their private life and their business:** fanatic discipline, empiric creativity, and productive paranoia.

6. **Discipline is not the same as hierarchical obedience or adherence to bureaucratic rules.** True discipline requires the independence of mind to reject pressure and conform in ways incompatible with value and performance standards, as well as the inner will to do what it takes to create a great outcome.

7. **Empirical creativity helps great leaders find a way out of difficult situations.** They engage directly with evidence, conduct practical experience, draw independent conclusions, and make bold and creative moves.

8. **Productive paranoia isn't just about avoiding danger.** Tenfold leaders turn hypervigilance into productive action, building cash reserves, developing new products, etc.

9. **Tenfold leaders are ambitious,** but for a purpose beyond themselves, be it building a great company or changing the world.

10. **The only type of failure that seals the fate of a company is Hitting the Death Line,** which means that if this happens, the company dies outright or becomes so damaged that it can no longer continue.

Great by Choice

Jim Collins, Morten Hansen

Great leaders know how to benefit even from problems and failures. Resilience, not luck, is the signature of greatness.

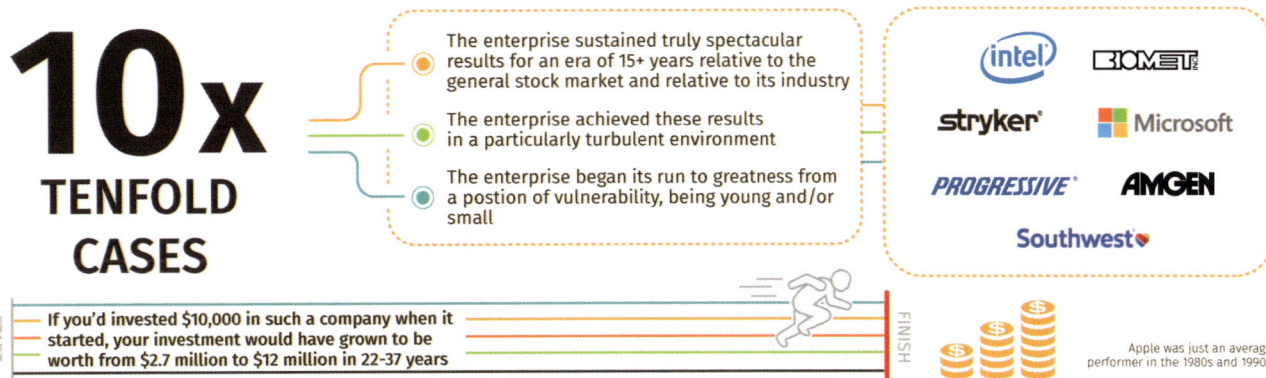

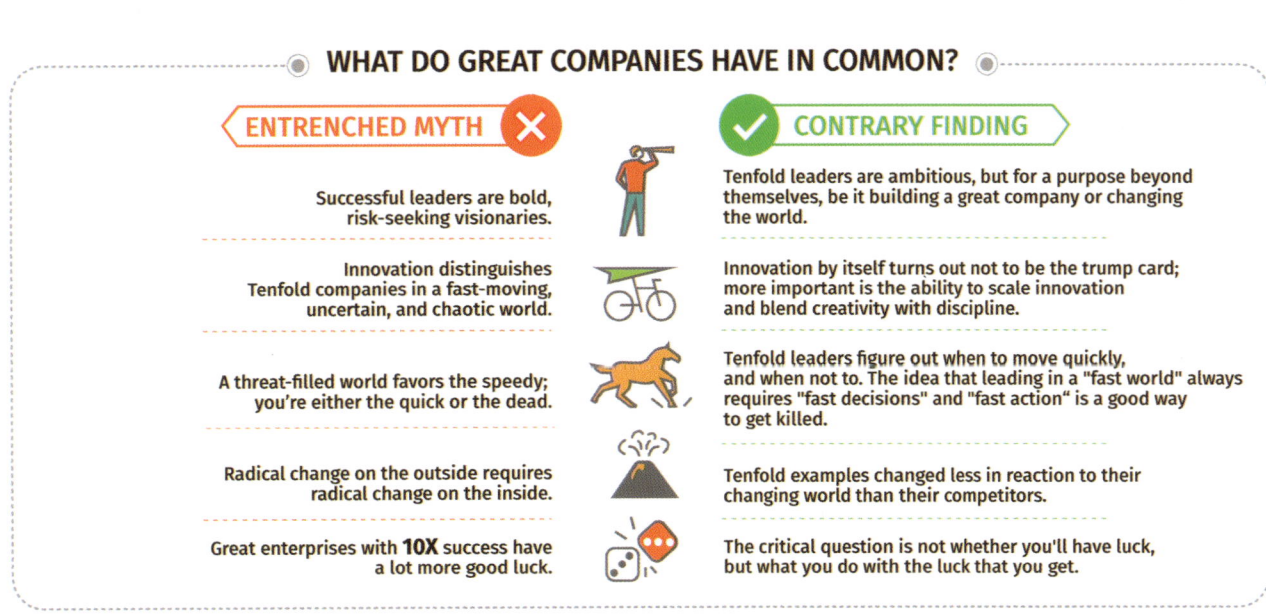

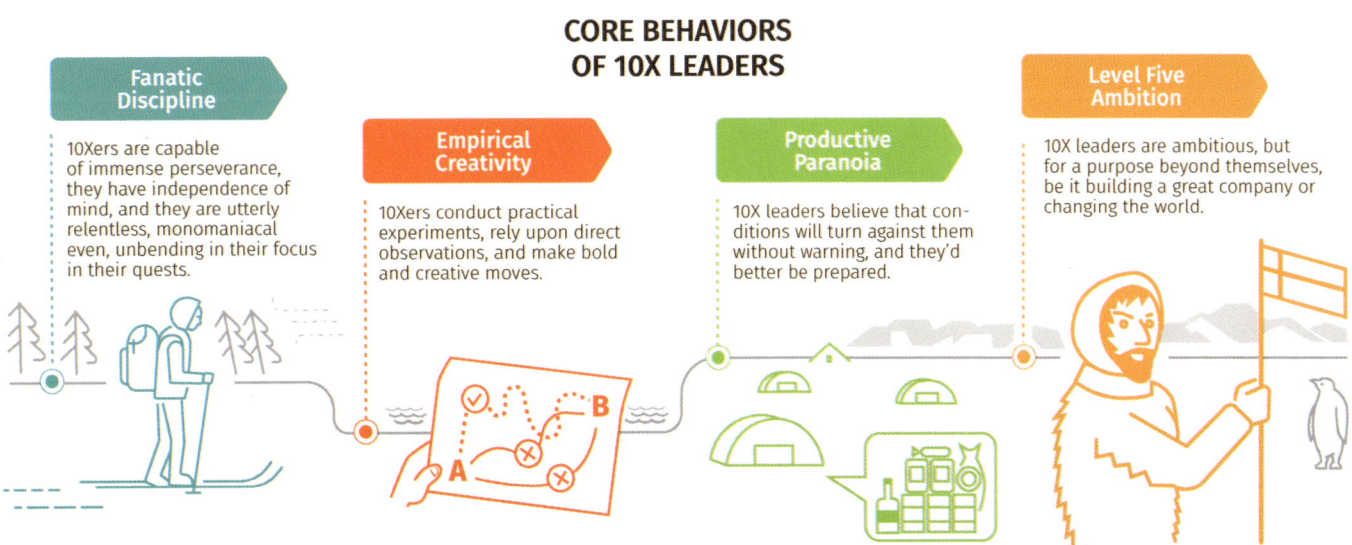

Personal development: 50 bestsellers in infographics

Great People Decisions: Why They Matter So Much, Why They Are So Hard, and How You Can Master Them

Claudio Fernández-Aráoz

1. **Hiring the right team is vital for a manager's success.** Assessing people correctly is a key managerial skill.

2. **Hiring an exceptional performer is a great piece of luck, because such people are few and far between.**

3. **The difficulty of performance evaluations, your own biases, misplaced incentives, and conflicts of interest can easily sabotage people decisions.**

4. **The higher the position, the more difficult it is to put together a standard set of required competences.** Some of the most common ones include being result-oriented, the ability to collaborate, develop people, and manage change.

5. **When making people decisions, make sure you consider the candidate's circumstances,** as they have a serious influence on the candidate's job decisions and the way he or she presents him/herself.

6. **Pay attention to the values and integrity of a candidate.** A company can teach people the necessary competencies, but it will not be able to build their character.

7. **Changes in teams are necessary not only in cases when performance falters,** but also when the team is facing macro-level forces or anticipating future challenges.

8. **In order to make the candidate selection process as efficient as possible, you need a clear sequence:** first produce a list of competencies required for the job; then, after analyzing the candidate's CV, structure the interview and reference checks to make sure the candidate possesses these competencies.

9. **After you have hired people, make sure there is proper team-building and integration in place.**

10. **Successful implementation of a strategy** requires having the right leaders and synching their activity on all levels of the corporate hierarchy.

Great People Decisions

Claudio Fernández-Aráoz

Personal success of a leader depends largely on his ability to get the right people and bring them together as a team.

WHEN IS CHANGE NEEDED?

 **Response to macro-level forces**
Globalization and rapid evolution of technology

 **Launching a new business**
Consider both internal promotions and outside hires

 **Performance problems**
Keep your eye on the real challenges and real solutions

 **Implementing new strategies**
A change in strategy has to ripple across multiple levels in a complex organization

 **Doing mergers and acquisitions**
Avoid playing politics or playing favorites

 **Anticipating future challenges**
Decide whether the right human resources are in place to deal with the future

BIASES TO AVOID

 Procrastination

 Overrating capability

 Snap judgements

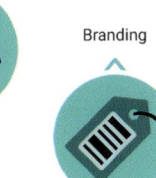 Branding

 Evaluating people in absolute terms

 Saving face

 Sticking with the familiar

 Emotional anchoring

TIPS TO CHOOSE THE BEST PEOPLE

 Figure out what you are looking for
- What skills and characteristics are required?
- How will the candidate actually perform?

Check whether the person has the required competencies
A structured interview is the best assessment method

Review candidates' prior performance
- Specific achievements and overall outcomes
- Reference check

Check what competencies were manifested in different circumstances
Are they in line with the competencies you require?

 Now you can predict candidates' performance on the job

MOTIVATE PROPERLY!

- Understand the main motives of the candidate. Ask yourself whether the proposed change is truly the best thing for him or her
- Share your passion about the opportunity
- Pay competitively for the relevant market
- Set up the right incentives with great care for their design
- Establish a culture that promotes the values of the company and people
- Provide support for integration and development in the candidate's new position

Reinventing Organizations

Frederic Laloux

1. **Most of present-day global corporations are Orange organizations.** They are focused on accountability, innovation and meritocracy ("power of merit").

2. **Dominant metaphors of the past, such as "Gang" (Red), "Army" (Orange), "Machine" (Amber) and "Family" (Green) are about to be succeeded by a new metaphor:** organizations as living systems (the color Teal).

3. **The transition to the Teal level will mean a revolutionary change of worldview.** People now understand for the first time that their paradigm includes all former paradigms.

4. **The core structural principles of Teal are decentralization, self-management and reduction of planning and controlling functions.**

5. **Wholeness practices in Teal organizations include taking values to the next level,** honoring all important commitments in people's lives, coaching, mentoring, and rejection of status attributes.

6. **For Teal organizations, the top priority is to pursue their evolutionary purpose,** while profit and a market share are a natural consequence of profound adherence to their values.

7. **There are two necessary conditions for organizations to make the leap to Teal structures and practices:** the top leader (or rather several leaders) must view the world through Teal lenses, and owners of the organization must also understand and embrace a Teal worldview.

8. **Self-management in a Teal organization is based on trust, data sharing, and each employee's responsibility.**

9. **The two pillars of a corporate culture in a Teal organization are:** the noble purpose of the organization, which everyone must share; and acknowledgement of every employee's value.

10. **Management of a Teal organization is carried out via role modeling:** the leader communicates values and preferred behaviors by his or her own example.

Reinventing Organizations

Frederic Laloux

Teal organizations correspond to the current stage of societal development and are based on decentralization and assigning responsibility to their people.

Green Pluralistic

The classic pyramidal structure is retained. Focus on culture and top-down empowerment to boost motivation

Culture-driven organizations, such as Southwest Airlines

- Empowerment
- Values-driven culture
- Stakeholder value

Teal Evolutionary

An evolving organization. Self-management in the framework of laws and evolutionary rules. The highest degree of freedom and responsibility for every person

- Self-management
- Wholeness
- Evolutionary purpose

Amber Impulsive

Clear ranks that stack up in an organizational pyramid. Top-down control over what is done and how it is done. Stable rituals and processes make life predictable

Church
Army
Government agencies
Schools and universities

- Stable organizational chart
- Replicable processes

Orange Achievement

Focus on beating competitors. Profit and growth. Innovation is key. Management by achieving objectives. Control over what is being done, freedom in how it is being done

Present-day global brands

- Innovation
- Accountability
- Meritocracy

Red Impulsive

The role of the chief is to enforce order. Fear keeps the organization under control. Short-term vision. Highly entrepreneurial in chaotic environments

Mafia
Street gangs

- Division of labor
- Top-down authority

Principles and Practices of Teal Organizations

Teal organizations operate without a power hierarchy

Self-management Practices
- Giving advice is more effective than giving orders.
- Everyone deserves respect, regardless of his or her position.
- Information is available to everyone.
- If there is a conflict, make your own decisions, but act in line with guidelines.
- Team outcomes must be clear.
- Dismissals are rare and decided by the team.
- Pay is discussed and decided by the team and the actual employee.

Wholeness Practices
- No undermining of the person's self-esteem.
- Attention to values.
- All employees have the same understanding of corporate culture.
- Office space is not assigned based on employee status.

Evolutionary Purpose Practices
- The company competes with the "old" mindset, not with other companies.
- The company cultivates open-mindedness.
- Trust your gut feeling
- Encouragement of spiritual practices
- Any employee can speak on behalf of the organization
- Active information exchange
- Attention to outside opportunities

Culture of Teal Organizations

- **Self-management based on trust, information sharing and all the employees' sharing responsibility**
- **Wholeness and acknowledgement of the value of every employee**
- **An evolutionary purpose shared by everyone**

Personal development: 50 bestsellers in infographics

My Years with General Motors

Alfred Sloan

1. **Coordinated decentralization saved General Motors, which was on the brink of a collapse in the 1920s.**

2. **Instead of a multitude of car models competing with each other, it was decided to create an inexpensive breakthrough car.**

3. **Problems with tests of a new air-cooled engine uncovered a conflict between line and division management.** It was resolved by putting together a committee that involved representatives of all key units.

4. **The basic elements of financial control in General Motors are** cost, price, volume, and rate of return on investment, which is used to measure the effectiveness of business-related decisions.

5. **Having achieved stability, the company added advisory groups as a new management level.** The General Technical Committee brought together financiers and administrators.

6. **Along with being concerned about return on shareholder value, the company strives to achieve sales and asset growth.** Being a market leader, General Motors makes sure it honors its commitments to employees, clients, dealers, suppliers and the community.

7. **General Motors has developed alongside the automotive industry and is always trying to be a leader.** Tough competition would sometimes force the company to reduce the lead time for developing new models. The company's current portfolio includes many overseas operations and models, as well as several nonautomotive ventures.

8. **Recruiting the best personnel is a key element of the HR policy in General Motors.** Benefits and bonuses provide for retaining and motivating top-class specialists.

9. **General Motors has developed accounting and management standards for its dealers that give them broader opportunities to generate profit.**

10. **The General Motors Acceptance Corporation (GMAC), a General Motors subsidiary, is a leading U. S. financial institution.** The corporation uses it to provide financing for its buyers. The GMAC was a pioneer in the U. S. consumer lending market.

My Years with General Motors

Alfred Sloan

The coordinated decentralization system developed by Alfred Sloan in the 1920s is still operating successfully.

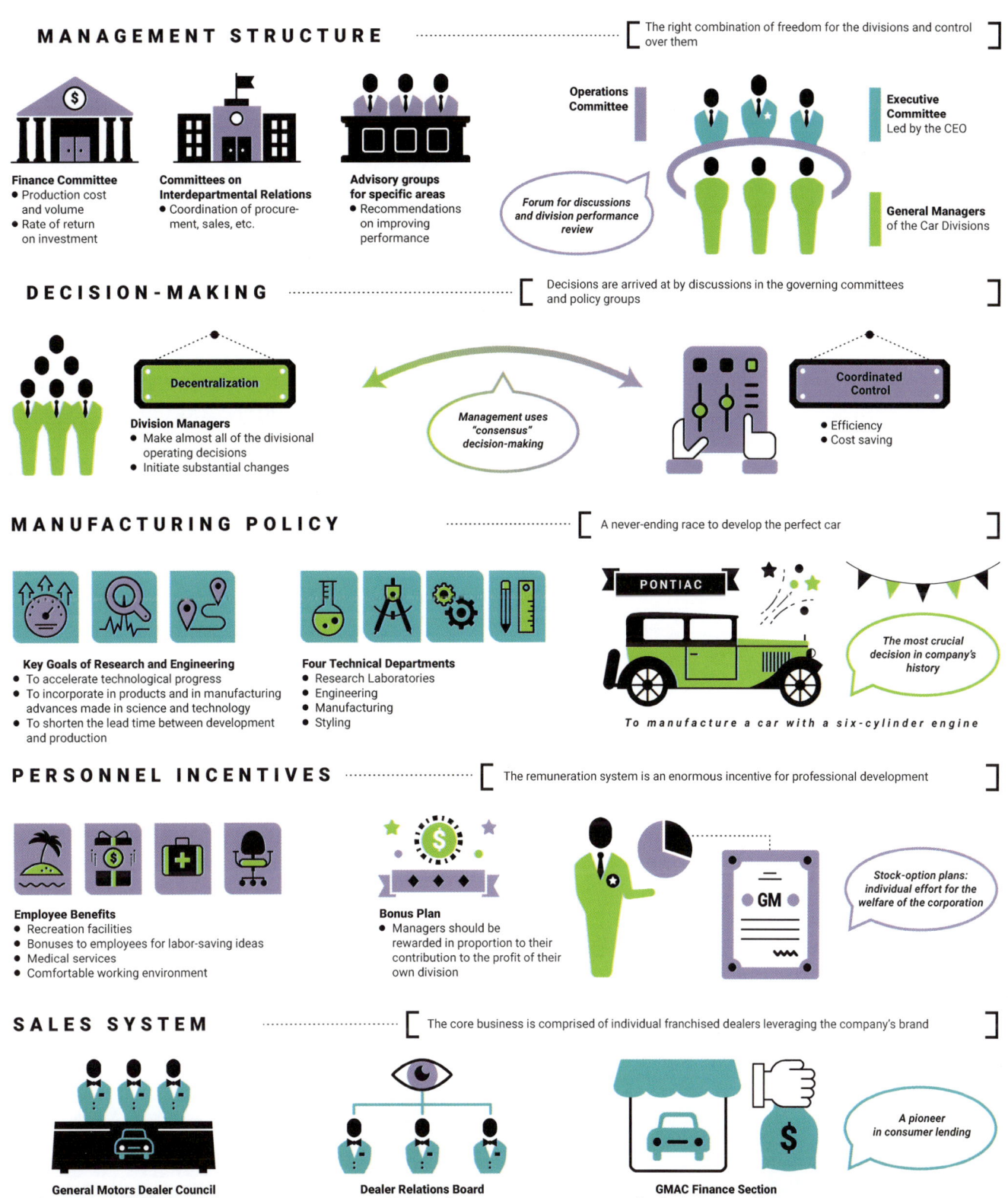

Personal development: 50 bestsellers in infographics

The Fifth Discipline.
The Art & Practice
of the Learning Organization

Peter Senge

1. **As standards of living grow, so do the ways people approach their work.** Now people want something more than to just earn money. They want their job to have meaning, to be involved in the process, and to take pride in its outcome.

2. **Organizations that excel today learn more quickly than their competitors,** have committed employees, allow them to participate in the decision-making, and are constantly undergoing change.

3. **Building a learning organization requires the mastery of five disciplines:** Personal Mastery, Mental Models, a Shared Vision, Team Learning, and Systems Thinking.

4. **The juxtaposition of vision (what we want) and a clear picture of current reality** (where we are relative to what we want) generates "creative tension" that fuels Personal Mastery.

5. **Mental Models can be simple generalizations or complex theories.** In any case, they shape how we act. It is important to be aware of existing mental models and to be able to build new ones.

6. **A vision is truly shared when all employees treat the common vision as their own.**

7. **Because two minds are better than one, Team Learning is aimed at tapping into the potential of many minds.** Its goals should be to achieve innovation but through thoroughly coordinated actions.

8. **The free flow of conflicting ideas is critically important for creative thinking** and discovering new solutions that no one individual could have uncovered on his or her own.

9. **Systems Thinking is a body of knowledge and tools that has been developed to allow people to see the world as a whole,** understand how certain elements are interconnected, and discover ways to make effective change.

10. **Building a learning organization is an ongoing process:** learning becomes a lifestyle that stimulates the efficient performance of a company and the personal growth of every team member.

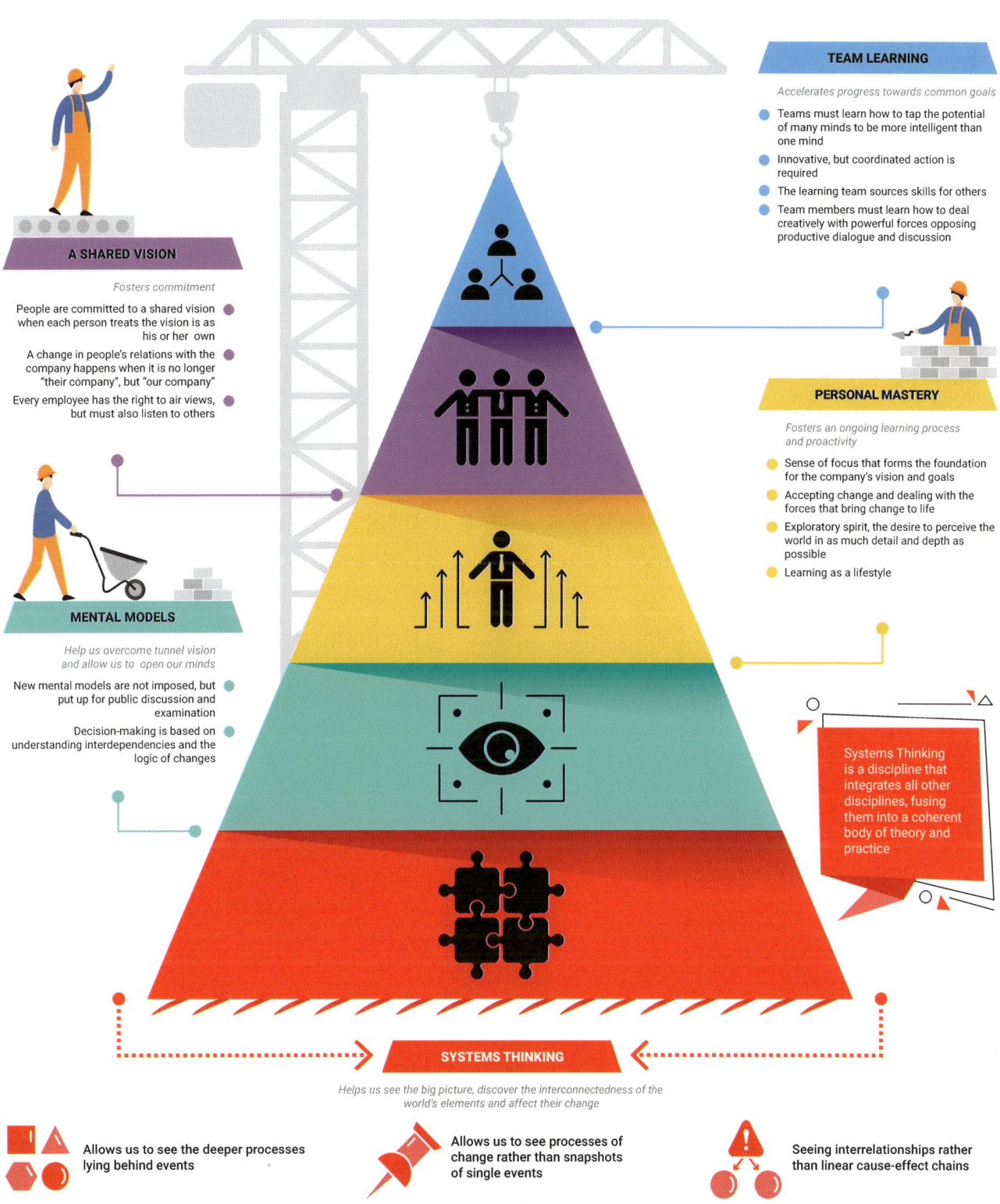

Chasing the Rabbit: How Market Leaders Outdistance the Competition and How Great Companies Can Catch Up and Win

Steven Spear

1. **All organizations have identical systems consisting of work, connections and routes.** Industry leaders, or the "rabbits" leading the pack, have a different approach to managing complex operations.

2. **High-velocity organizations are focused on the integration** of specialties into a whole process and always concerned about how the work of individuals and teams contributes to (or impedes) the process of which they are a part.

3. **In high-speed organizations, successful employees are those who think critically and complete tasks earlier than planned.**

4. **Leaders of high-velocity organizations want to understand and solve problems, not put up with them;** they do not encourage workarounds.

5. **High-velocity organizations do not make distinctions between "normal" operations and "crisis" response;** crisis recovery is part of their system.

6. **High-velocity organizations insist that "the scientific method" be used in solving problems in a disciplined fashion;** it reflects the conviction that when something is changed, those making the alteration should have a clear idea of what actions are expected and what outcomes they can expect.

7. **If employees of a high-velocity organizations succeed, they win.** If they do not, they learn how to succeed next time, and that is also a win.

8. **When people in a high-velocity organization begin to do their work, they do so with the cumulative experience of everyone in the organization who has ever done the same work.** Nobody has to start from scratch.

9. **Regardless of the industry, leading companies possess the following four capabilities:** they shape design to capture existing problems; they swarm and solve problems to build new knowledge; they share new knowledge new knowledge throughout the organization; they lead the pack by developing capabilities 1, 2, and 3.

10. **If you want to create a high-velocity organization, start with a relatively small team, focus on solving a problem that really matters.** Make sure that every layer of management is involved, budget time every day to analyze achievements and failures, share what you have learned with others, and be prepared for errors.

Chasing the Rabbit

Steven Spear

All organizations are alike. A school, a hospital, and a nuclear power plant are identical systems that consist of work, connections, and routes. Industry leaders, or the "rabbits" running ahead of the pack, have a different approach to managing complex operations.

TRADITIONAL COMPANIES (LOW-VELOCITY)		VS		HIGH-VELOCITY COMPANIES
Lack of alignment, bureaucratic delays, difficulties with getting approvals		STRUCTURE		Managing the functions as part of the process
Unwillingness to change outdated working methods		DYNAMICS		Continually improving the pieces and the process
Processes are so poorly designed that problems are bandaged and worked around and are sure to pop up again		CRISIS RESPONSE		The only difference between glitches and crises is one of scale and immediacy, not approach

CAPABILITIES OF HIGH-VELOCITY ORGANIZATIONS

1 Specifying a design to capture existing problems and building in tests to reveal problems — Integration, efficiency

2 Swarming and solving problems to build new knowledge — Management, self-improvement

3 Sharing new knowledge throughout the organization

4 Leadership

TIPS TO BUILD AND MAINTAIN A HIGH-VELOCITY ORGANIZATION

- Start with a small team
- Solve a problem that really matters
- Make sure that every layer of management is involved
- Don't think too much, but always be doing something
- Be prepared for errors
- Budget time every day for designing a work process
- Share what you learn with others

CRISIS RESPONSE

- Processes are detailed in a methodical fashion while they are being designed
- Constant attention to deviations
- When perturbations are experienced, they are swarmed and investigated
- Problem solving through high-speed cycles of discovery
- When discoveries are made, there is an organization-wide protocol for sharing them

TOYOTA designed a system that can transform any organization into a high-velocity organization

Creativity, Inc.: Overcoming the Unseen Forces That Stand in the Way of True Inspiration

Amy Wallace, Edwin Catmull

1 **As the leader of a creative team, your task is to create a fertile environment and to keep it healthy.** There are active steps you can take to protect the creative process and remove the blocks that get in the way.

2 **Getting the team right is the necessary precursor to getting the ideas right.** Getting the right people and the right chemistry is more important than getting the right idea.

3 **Make failure into something people can face without fear.** Mistakes aren't a necessary evil; they are an inevitable consequence of doing something new.

4 **Create an environment of openness and sincerity and encourage the open exchange of opinions.**

5 **Criticism must be productive.** Teach your employees to discuss an idea or product, not the person behind it.

6 **Protect new ideas from those who fear change: many people will resist changes with all their might.**

7 **Trying to make processes better, easier, and cheaper is an important aspiration, but it is not the goal.** Making something great is the goal.

8 **Do not foster unhealthy work addictions.** The best producers are those who observe a life-work balance.

9 **Get rid of unnecessary rules and limitations.** Abandoning them requires more attention from management but will create an atmosphere of freedom and creativity in the company.

10 **Every person is a creator.** By helping people develop their creative abilities, you do something good for them and the company.

Creativity, Inc.

Amy Wallace, Edwin Catmull

As co-founder of Pixar, Ed Catmull smashed multiple stereotypes about animation and CGI. His new dream is to use his experience in managing creative teams to smash stereotypes about management.

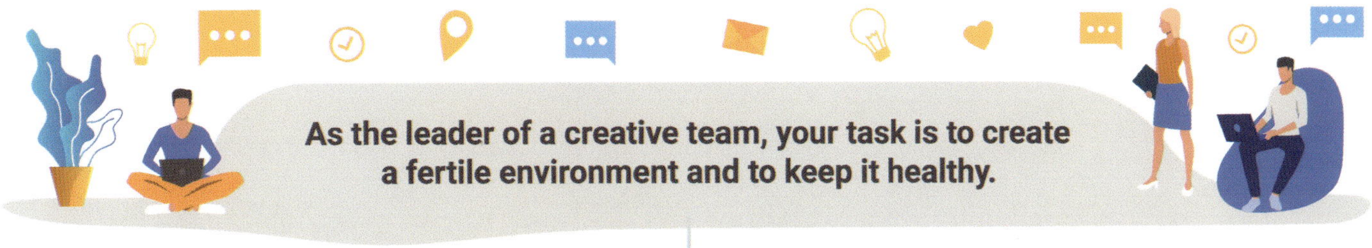

As the leader of a creative team, your task is to create a fertile environment and to keep it healthy.

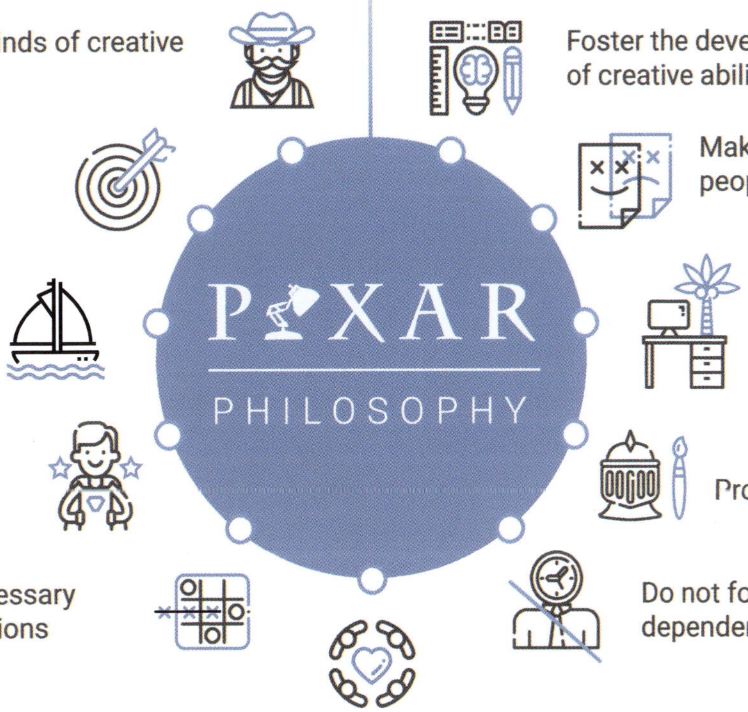

PIXAR PHILOSOPHY

- Encourage all kinds of creative expression
- The goal is making something great
- While you are floating with the tide, retain control of the work process
- Hire the best people
- Get rid of unnecessary rules and limitations
- Foster the development of creative abilities
- Make failure into something people can face without fear
- The workplace should be a specific creative cuture
- Protect new ideas
- Do not foster unhealthy work dependence

Make sure the teams you put together have the right chemistry

Braintrust: Unique Pixar Feature

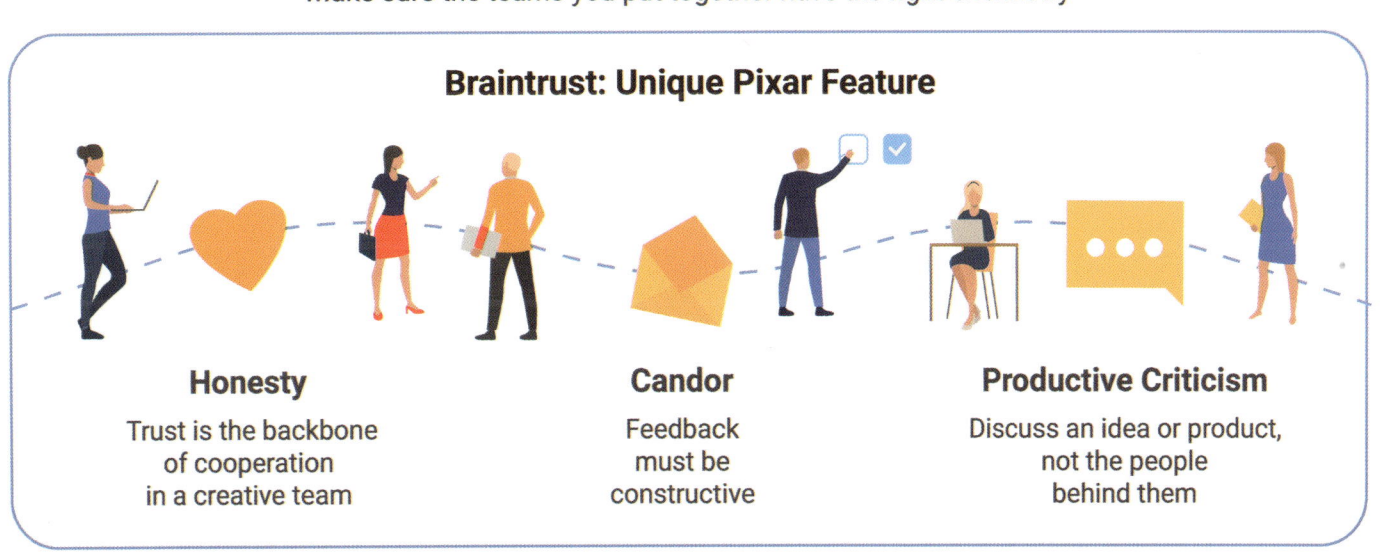

Honesty
Trust is the backbone of cooperation in a creative team

Candor
Feedback must be constructive

Productive Criticism
Discuss an idea or product, not the people behind them

How The Mighty Fall: And Why Some Companies Never Give In

Jim Collins

1. **Every institution is vulnerable, no matter how great it is.** Anyone can fail.

2. **Institutional decline happens in five stages:** Hubris Born of Success, Undisciplined Pursuit of More, Denial of Risk and Peril, Grasping for Salvation, and Capitulation to Irrelevance or Death.

3. **A crisis can be prevented if declining systems are detected in time.** As long as a company has not reached the fifth, terminal stage, decline can be reversed.

4. **Don't overestimate your own merit and capabilities.** Luck and chance play a role in many successful outcomes.

5. **Focus on current profitability:** it is the only way to retain management control over costs.

6. **Don't blame external factors for setbacks.** Don't discount negative data. Make sure you and your reports accept responsibility for negative outcomes.

7. **If everyone is convinced that difficulties are "cyclic" or "not that bad," you will not be able to detect and fix their underlying causes.**

8. **Hasty, reactive behavior may bring about the very outcomes you most fear.** Resist making decisions during panic.

9. **Don't grasp for a silver bullet.** In a time of crisis, there is not much to benefit from restructuring, new product launches, appointment of new charismatic leaders or capturing new markets.

10. **Rebuilding a company requires staying loyal to corporate principles and values,** getting back to solid management disciplines, using rational management methods and the belief that the company will be able to become great and thrive again.

How The Mighty Fall

Jim Collins

The process of decline is never sudden. Timely "diagnostics" will help the company avoid spending money and time looking for ways to save the company.

REQUIREMENTS FOR STABILITY

- Rigorous strategic thinking
- Solid management discipline
- Flexibility and ability to change tactics at the right moment
- Never giving up on the core purpose of the company

FIVE STAGES OF DECLINE

Self-diagnostic checklist

1. HUBRIS BORN OF SUCCESS

- ☑ Success entitlement, arrogance
- ☐ "What" replaces "why"
- ☐ Neglect for learning and development
- ☐ Discounting the role of luck
- ☐ Growing too quickly or a change in direction

Striving for self-improvement is the only path forward to achieve the company's development.

"What if we were just really lucky or in the right place at the right time?"

Managers are no longer able to assess properly what they can and wish to do.

"What are the key posts in your organization? What are your backup plans should a key person leave a key post?"

2. UNDISCIPLINED PURSUIT OF MORE

- Unsustainable quest for growth ☐
- Declining proportion of the right people at key posts ☐
- People in power allocate more for themselves ☐
- Easy cash erodes cost discipline ☐
- Failure to groom excellent leaders from within ☐
- Bureaucracy subverts discipline ☐

3. DENIAL OF RISK AND PERIL

- ☐ Amplify the positive, discard the negative
- ☐ Obsessive reorganizations
- ☐ Erosion of healthy team dynamics
- ☐ Incurring huge downside risk based on ambiguous data
- ☐ Privileged position of company leadership

Managers tend to discount or explain away negative data, while they highlight and amplify external praise.

"Is this team still capable of going up, or is it pulling the company down?"

Lurching for a silver bullet to bring quick relief

"Is there a chance to get back to the disciplines that made the company great and successful in the first place?"

4. GRASPING FOR SALVATION

- Grasping for a leader-as-savior (mostly an outside savior) ☐
- A leap into a new strategy or an exciting innovation ☐
- Radical change and "revolution" with fanfare ☐
- A "game-changing" merger or acquisition ☐
- People cannot easily articulate what the company stands for ☐

5. CAPITULATION TO IRRELEVANCE OR DEATH

☠ Terminal stage for any business

- ⚑ Dramatic loss of a market share
- ⚑ Sale of the company
- ⚑ Bankruptcy

The Dance of Change: The Challenges to Sustaining Momentum in a Learning Organization

Peter Senge, George Roth

1. **If you don't have enough time, develop your planning capabilities.** Manage your time rather than skip out on innovation programs.

2. **Make sure a proper mentoring system is in place in the company, and develop a culture where seeking help is welcomed, not viewed as a sign of weakness.**

3. **Line managers are responsible for building a connection between routine employee tasks and the global goals of the company.** They must promote the effectiveness of programs for change and demonstrate how this will improve the "living quality" of the organization.

4. **Managers are fully responsible for building the credibility of organizational values by example, not by articulation.** In order to support top-down initiatives, employees must believe that their boss walks the talk.

5. **Fear is a natural response to the precariousness of a changing situation.** Create a safe environment and don't lash out at your subordinates if you see they are being too anxious, or you may demotivate them even more.

6. **A new approach to doing business requires new metrics.** Reconsider your definitions of failure and success. Appreciate the time delays that are involved in profound change.

7. **Any plan for change has True-Believers and Non-Believers.** Become "bi-cultural" and work to make the corporate culture more flexible.

8. **A conflict between power groups is as inevitable as confrontation between True-Believers and Non-Believers.** Respect other people's boundaries and hold tight once you have chosen your strategy: if you have decided in favor of decentralization, don't go back to the prior previous structure.

9. **Strive for maximum transparency of borders within the organization, engage network leaders as carriers of new ideas and as mentors, and design more effective media for internal information exchange.**

10. **Use creative, outside-the-box thinking, engage people to propose their vision of the company's global goals and strategies for the company.** Develop a service attitude, i. e., serve your colleagues, rivals, and the world, as part of your organization's ethics and practices.

The Dance of Change

Peter Senge, George Roth

The harder the push for transformation, the stronger the resistance. Don't wait for underwater rocks to come to the surface, take measures to prevent potential issues before they emerge.

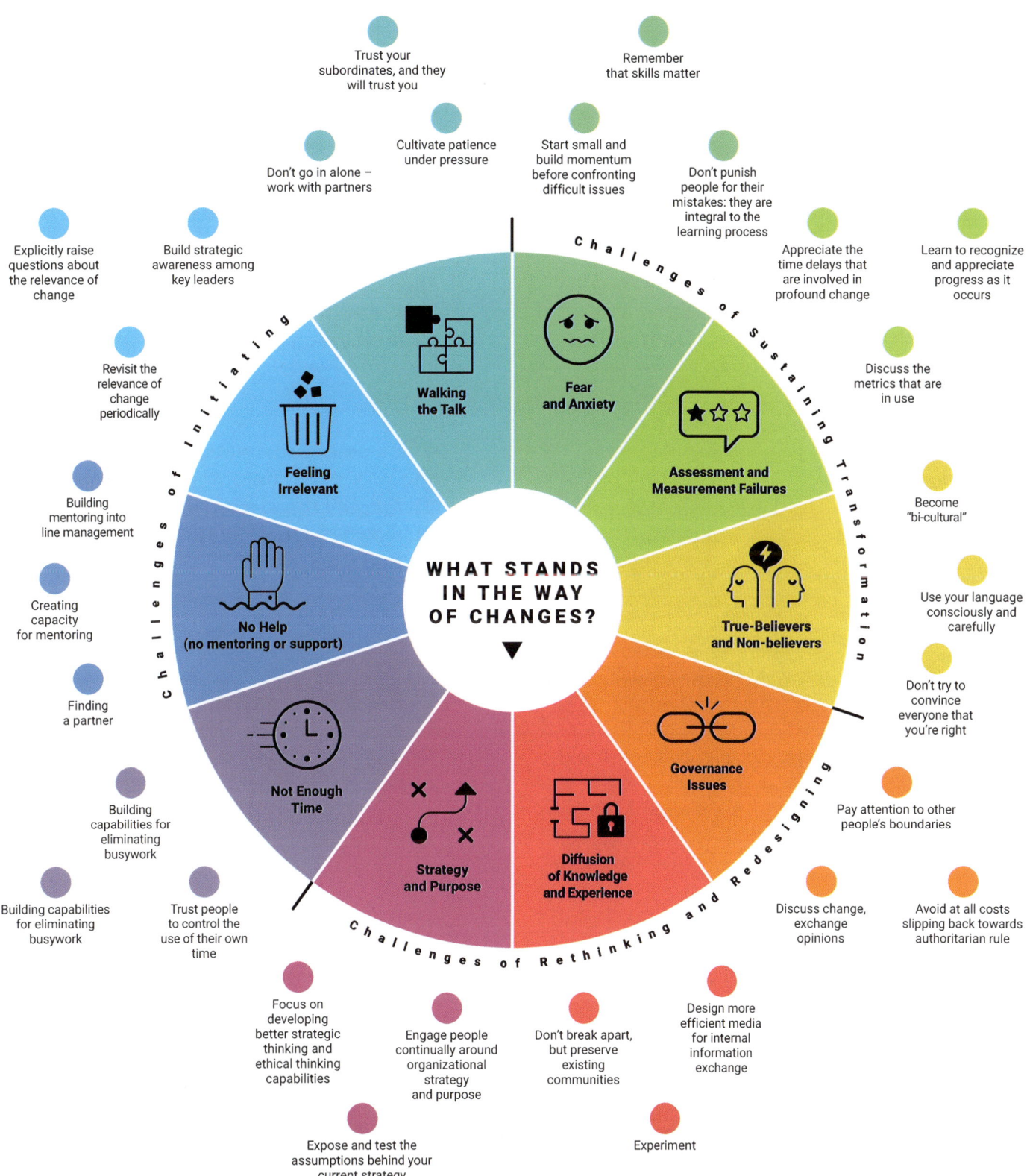

The Goal: A Process of Ongoing Improvement

Eliyahu Goldratt, Jeff Cox

1) There are just three measurements that are central to knowing if a company is making money: net profit, return on investment, and cash flow.

2) In order to assess daily operations of a manufacturing organization, a set of three measurements is required: throughput (the rate at which the system generates money through sales), inventory, and operational expense (the money the system spends to turn inventory into throughput).

3) The main goal of any manufacturing company is to earn money by increasing throughput while simultaneously reducing both inventory and operating expenses. Every action that does not bring the company to its goal is not productive.

4) The task of a manager is to balance capacity, workload, and personnel engagement so that the system will have no idle time and will not generate extra operational expense that is not offset by actual sales.

5) An hour lost due to a bottleneck is an hour lost for the entire system.

6) An hour saved at a non-bottleneck is a mirage.

7) Bottlenecks govern both throughput and inventory.

8) Evaluate manufacturing company performance using financial measurements, not capacity utilization rates.

9) The constraint-based process of manufacture management is as follows:
1) Identify the system's bottlenecks;
2) Decide how to fix or eliminate the bottlenecks;
3) Subordinate everything else to the above decision;
4) Elevate the system's bottlenecks;
5) If in previous steps a bottleneck has been eliminated go back to step one.

10) Do not allow inertia to cause new constraints.

The Goal

Eliyahu Goldratt, Jeff Cox

Eliyahu Goldratt developed the theory of constraints, which has changed the rules of manufacturing process management worldwide. His work has made it clear that the current system of measurements is a roadblock standing in the way of making manufacturing operations profitable, and this must change.

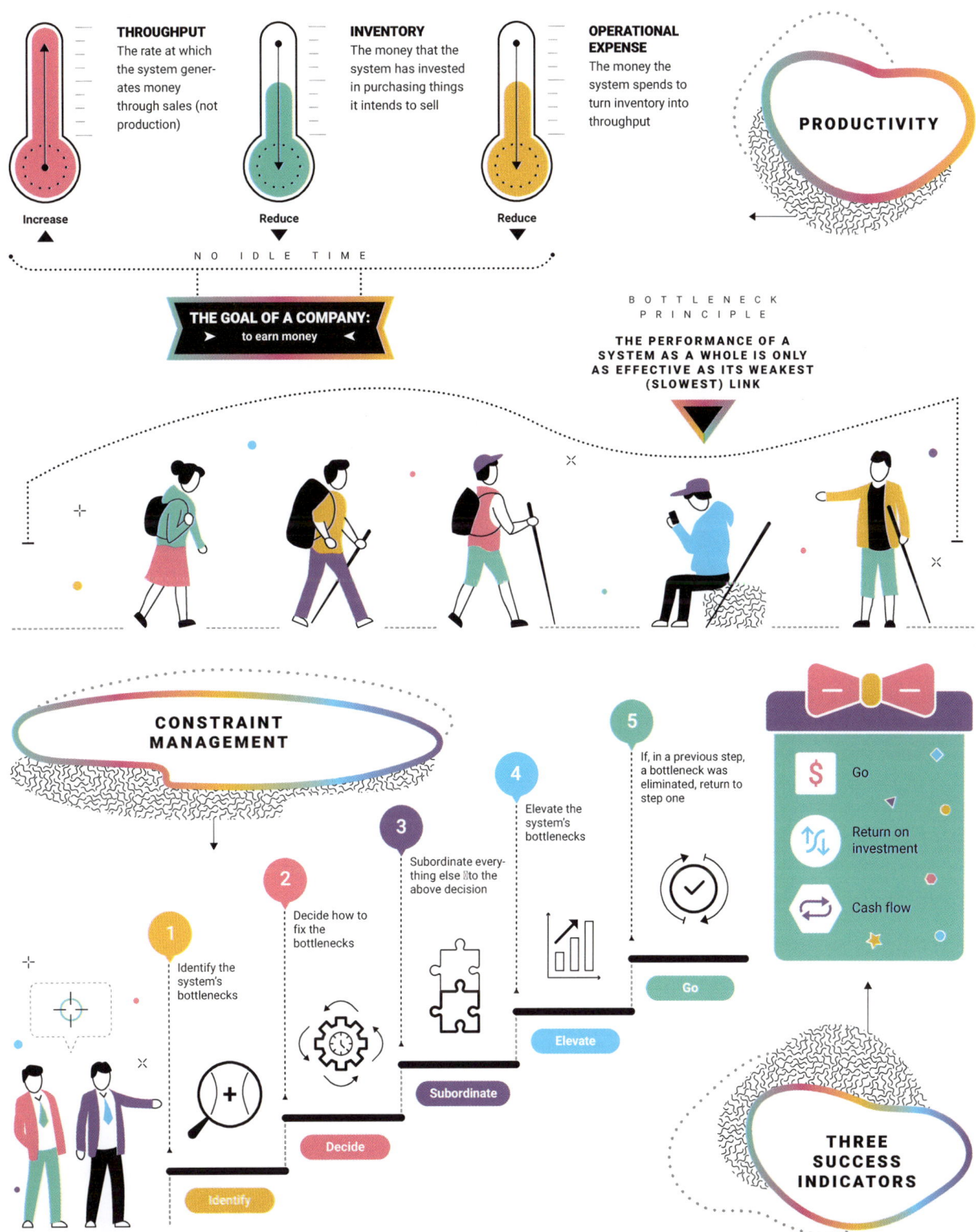

How Google Works

Eric Schmidt, Jonathan Rosenberg

1. **In order to attract and keep the best talent you need great ideas and a strong strategic foundation that the company's founder's stand behind.** Then the team will get behind them. They will become a benchmark for strategic and tactical decisions.

2. **The key function of company leaders in the Internet age is to find and hire the right people, so-called "smart creatives".** But it is up to all team members to look for talent.

3. **Smart creatives need an environment where they can feed and stimulate their creativity.** Offer them opportunities to learn and share knowledge, give them new challenges.

4. **Smart creatives do not put up with red tape or being bossed around —** decisions should be quick and based on facts and objective data.

5. **If you want better performance from the best, celebrate and reward them disproportionately.**

6. **Working in the office encourages interaction between employees, therefore working from home should be discouraged.** However, employees should have flexible working hours.

7. **The person running an innovative company should have a product background and be a great communicator and information router.**

8. **For something to be innovative it needs to offer new functionality (technical insight), but it also has to be surprising to the user.** Give consumers something they had no idea existed and solve a problem that they will only find out about tomorrow.

9. **Don't follow the competition.** This creates a never-ending spiral into mediocrity.

10. **Google is just one of numerous possible success stories.** Find your specialization, your path and devise your own methods. Then engage smart creatives and work as hard as you can.

How Google Works

Eric Schmidt, Jonathan Rosenberg

What is the secret of Google's success? How has the company managed to stay among the world's most attractive employers for many years in a row? This is an inspiring success story from where there is a lot to learn and a lot of insights to use in your own business and career.

GOOGLE'S OFFICES
Everything you might need for comfortable and relaxed work: the best equipment, free lunches, dry cleaning, fitness centers, discount massages

SMART CREATIVE

- Doesn't just design concepts, builds prototypes
- Combines technical depth with business savvy
- Dress code? He must wear something

- A firehouse of new ideas
- Curious
- Self-directed
- Risk taker
- Collaborates freely
- The bigger the impact, the bigger the compensation

TOP MANAGER

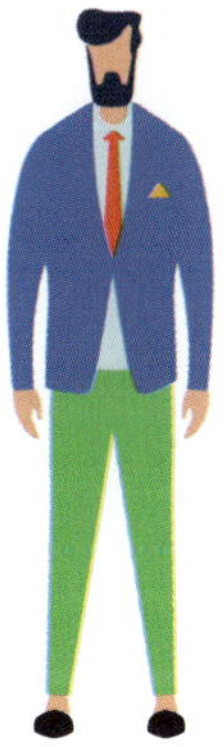

1. Spends **80%** of his time on **80%** of his revenue
2. Holds himself to objectively high standards as a manager
3. Cannot stand red tape or being bossed around
4. Accepts help from his mentor
5. A great communicator and information router
6. Has a product background

MAKING DECISIONS

- Come to the best idea for the company
- Dissent must be an obligation, not an option
- Be especially aware of quiet people – they may be of the shy but brilliant type

- Make it safe to ask tough questions and bear bad news
- Decisions must be based on correct data
- Every meeting needs a single owner

GOOGLE PRINCIPLES

Outrun technological progress
Give customers today what they will only need tomorrow

Find your area and excel at it
Google chose to focus on Internet searches

The people who run the company should be product people
Even a domain expert should have business savvy

Focus on breakthrough technologies
Top propriety products for development

Don't follow the competition
Think of a need that you and the competition haven't met yet

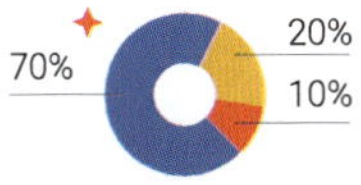

Investing rule
- Core businesses 70%
- Emerging products that achieved some early success 20%
- New things that have the risk of failure but a big payoff if successful 10%

User convenience and values
Offer people easy access to a high-quality product, and money will follow

Don't be evil, make the world a better place
Google is a cultural beacon for preserving trust, especially given the volumes of users' personal data they store

Personal development: 50 bestsellers in infographics

The Tiredness Cure. How to Beat Fatigue and Feel Great for Good

Sohere Roked

1. **Integrative (or holistic) medicine views the human body as a whole** and considers nutrition, physical fitness, stress levels, digestive system performance, chemical and hormonal balance.

2. **You must take responsibility for your own health and become the best expert on you.**

3. **Genes change throughout human life.** Telomeres, which are sequences located at the termini of linear chromosomes and responsible for health and longevity, can be enlarged if you take care of your health on a regular basis.

4. **To keep fatigue away and feel full of vitality for life, there are four key components you must strive towards: good nutrition, removal of vices, stress management, and exercise.**

5. **A number of health problems can be caused by acidity in the body.** The main causes of acidification are thought to be smoking and a diet that is rich in acidifying foods such as grains, alcohol, coffee, tea, refined sugars and processed food, and low in alkalizing foods such as fruit and vegetables. Stress and a lack of physical activity can also cause acidification.

6. **The simplest way to see if you are experiencing intolerance to a product** is to cut it out of your life for two weeks and see how you feel.

7. **Avoid food that is grown and processed with the use of chemicals.**

8. **Eat a minimum of five fruit and vegetables a day.** Drink more water.

9. **Try to leave at least 12 hours between your evening meal and morning meal.**

10. **Learn to meditate, master relaxation techniques, practice yoga, swim, walk or do pilates.**

The Tiredness Cure

Sohere Roked

To keep fatigue at bay and feel full of vitality for life, there are four key components you must strive towards: good nutrition, no vices, stress management, and exercise.

BECOME THE EXPERT ON YOU

NUTRITION

- Eat 400 g of fruit and vegetables a day
- Drink more water
- Take multivitamins
- Pay attention to calories (100 kcal in a portion of broccoli is more healthful than 100 kcal in a cookie)
- Limit your intake of tea, coffee, alcohol, grains, sugar and processed food
- Avoid: food exposed to chemicals
- food to which you have an intolerance

EXERCISE

- Exercise can be a walk; using the stairs; cycling to work; or swimming
- Spend 10 minutes a day exercising
- It can be damaging to do intensive exercises when you are feeling weak
- Avoid heavy loads without proper preparation

GOOD SLEEP

- Products improving your chances of getting a good night's sleep: non-dairy milk, nuts, bananas, spinach, chickpea, and salmon
- Go to bed and wake up as per schedule
- Don't stick to an old mattress or pillow
- Turn off your smartphone/computer an hour before you go to bed;
- Have a hot bath;
- Make sure your room is dark, quiet, and cool

MANAGING STRESS

- Value what you have
- Set aside some time for yourself
- Stay away from people who ruin your self-esteem
- Take time off from work and your routine
- Do yoga
- Eat healthfully
- Spend time relaxing

TAKE RESPONSIBILITY FOR YOUR WELL-BEING

Why Zebras Don't Get Ulcers: The Acclaimed Guide to Stress, Stress-Related Diseases, and Coping

Robert Sapolsky

1 **In times of stress, the body must release as much energy as possible and channel it to vital organs.** Some processes accelerate at the expense of others.

2 **The effects of stress pose less danger** than reducing them in the wrong way (comfort foods, acts of aggression, etc.).

3 **Stressors:** fear, anger, pain, high physical and mental tension, insufficient sleep, guilt, loss of control, social isolation, hunger, poverty.

4 **In children, high levels of stress are caused by a lack of physical contact with or attention from adults.** The stress experienced by a pregnant female affects her fetus too.

5 **Ulcers are the most frequent consequence of stress.** Others include insulin resistance, diabetes, obesity, high blood pressure, suppressed immunity or autoimmune diseases, as well as the impairment of intelligence, memory and libido.

6 **Fear of aging and dying is typical for success-oriented cultures.** The truth is that elderly people are often happier than young people.

7 **Stress reduction factors include: moderate amounts of food and drinks;** breathing exercises; adequate physical exercises; hobbies, reading, daydreaming; one-off acts of agression, tenderness, solace, and social support.

8 **The people who cope with stress most efficiently** are those who work a lot, are responsible, are in the higher levels of hierarchy (but not at the top), have many friends and relatives, regularly exercise and have hobbies.

9 **The optimal strategy for dealing with stress is being flexible.** Learn to recognize your stressors and focus on ways to cope with the physical ones. As for psychological stressors, it is better to just let them be.

10 **Dealing with stress must not become your primary goal, otherwise it will become a stressor in and of itself.**

Why Zebras Don't Get Ulcers

Robert Sapolsky

The optimal strategy for dealing with stress is being flexible and learning to recognize the various stressors you face. Your focus should be on responding as much as possible to actual physical stress. As for the games your mind plays with you, just let them be.

How to Stay Sane

Philippa Perry

1. **The foundations of our emotional constitution are poured when we are children.** But the structure can be altered at any time throughout our lives.

2. **Self-observation teaches us not to be taken over by obsessive thoughts and feelings.** With self-observation we develop more internal clarity, become more open and empathetic, get a better understanding of ourselves and rid ourselves of toxic thoughts.

3. **Mental health and happiness primarily depend on how we relate to others.** Maintaining social contact is a must for mental health.

4. **Having meaningful communication with people starts with being open and allowing yourself to be your true self, not who you think you should be.** If we do not allow ourselves to feel vulnerable, we deny ourselves the opportunity to experience genuine dialogue.

5. **Learning new things all the time makes the brain plastic and helps us maintain social connections and deal with our problems.**

6. **Physical exercises supplies oxygen to the brain, and the more oxygen it gets, the better it functions.**

7. **Optimists are more likely to trust others and therefore enjoy more satisfying relationships.** Optimistic people recover more quickly after operations and have higher survival rates after cancer. Optimism puts you in a better mood and thereby decreases stress.

8. **Identify mental lenses that define your view of reality.** Edit the narratives that you tell yourself, adding more light and benevolence to them.

9. **When you make a genogram, you uncover the characteristics you inherited from your family, especially from those who were around you during your childhood.** The point of this exercise is to release you from this inheritance so you can become more independent.

10. **Successful therapy is about improving your self-observation abilities, the way you relate to others, and the way you deal with stress.** It also allows you to rewrite your self-narratives, create new meaning, and imagine different endings.

How to Stay Sane

Philippa Perry

Practice self-observation, be kind to others, master new skills, be optimistic, and don't forget about exercising — this keeps mental issues away.

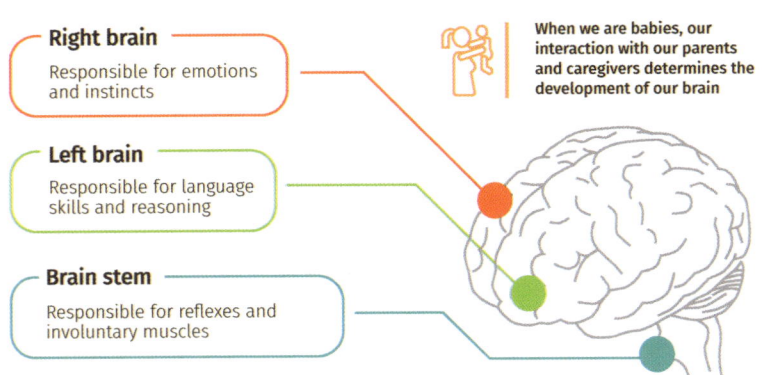

Right brain
Responsible for emotions and instincts

Left brain
Responsible for language skills and reasoning

Brain stem
Responsible for reflexes and involuntary muscles

When we are babies, our interaction with our parents and caregivers determines the development of our brain

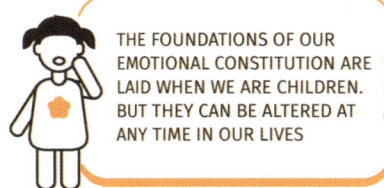

THE FOUNDATIONS OF OUR EMOTIONAL CONSTITUTION ARE LAID WHEN WE ARE CHILDREN. BUT THEY CAN BE ALTERED AT ANY TIME IN OUR LIVES

The right brain develops by the time we are two years old and keeps on controlling us throughout our lives

SUSTAINING MENTAL HEALTH

Self-observation

Self-observation teaches us not to be taken over by obsessive, toxic thoughts and feelings. With self-observation we develop more internal clarity and become more open to the emotional lives of those around us

- What am I feeling now?
- What am I thinking now?
- What am I doing at this moment?
- How am I breathing?
- What do I want for myself in the next moment?

When we become more sensitive towards ourselves and more knowledgeable about our own feelings, we are more able to tap into, and empathize with, the feelings of other people.

Relating to Others

Meaningful communication with people starts with being open. Allow yourself to be your true self and not who you think you should be

- Maintain a balance between egoism and altruism
- Be open about your moods, feelings, and thoughts
- Share objective information
- A good relationship is about finding a way forward together
- Support the people you are close to, try not to criticize them

Stress

Moderate levels of stress keep our minds in condition. The "good stress" promotes the neural growth hormones that support learning

- Find something genuinely new to do
- Devote much attention to it
- Be emotionally engaged
- Give it up only if you see that it gets you nowhere

Learning gives us food for thought, leaving less time for boredom and depression.

Personal Narrative

If we get to know the stories we live by, we will be able to edit and change them if we need to

- Set your "filters" to objective information
- Add new meaning to your narratives
- Create a genogram: analyze the behaviors and nature of your relatives

If you can dream and escape into your imagination, it will help you cope with unbearable situations in the real world.

Exercise

- Delivers oxygen to the brain
- Reduces age-related brain degeneration
- Helps you avoid depression

Optimism

Focuses on positive outcomes of events you are going through. Optimism puts you in a better mood and helps you live longer

Personal development: 50 bestsellers in infographics

The Power of Full Engagement. Managing Energy, Not Time, Is the Key to High Performance and Personal Renewal

Jim Loehr, Tony Schwartz

1. **Contrary to popular belief, it is energy, not time, that is our most precious resource in present-day realities.** A perfect schedule is useless when your energy level is at zero.

2. **Full engagement requires drawing on four separate, but related sources of energy: physical, emotional, mental, and spiritual.** By balancing energy expenditure with intermittent energy renewal, we can build our energy "muscles."

3. **Physical energy is the fundamental source of fuel for other energy dimensions, primarily emotional and mental energy.**

4. **Breathing, eating, water, and sleep are key to maintaining physical energy.** Follow the natural rhythms of activity and recovery. Choose exercises that imply heart rate variability (higher-lower-higher).

5. **In order to ignite our emotional energy levels, we must do things that make us self-confident and give us joy, such as gaining new experience, socializing, and developing hobbies and artistic abilities.** The key "muscles", or competencies, that fuel positive emotions are empathy, self-control, self-confidence, and a readiness to manage negative emotions.

6. **Maximum mental capacity is derived from challenging the brain,** retaining realistic optimism, and maintaining a balance between expanding and recovering mental energy.

7. **Spiritual energy provides a force for action in all other dimensions of our lives.** The key muscle that serves spiritual energy is character, which can be improved at any age. Prayer, retreat, concentration, and meditation, as well as altruism, are all a means to sustain our spiritual energy levels.

8. **Energy capacity diminishes with both overuse and underuse.**

9. **We must learn to balance between energy expenditure and intermittent energy renewal.**

10. **People who oscillate between high positive energy (work/engagement) and low positive energy (rest/recovery) demonstrate the highest performance levels.**

The Power of Full Engagement

Jim Loehr, Tony Schwartz

Human beings are complex energy systems, in which four dynamics interact to give us energy.
To perform at our best, we must skillfully manage each of these interconnected dimensions of energy.

Mental Energy

To perform at our best, we need access to realistic optimism, which implies seeing the world as it is, but always working positively towards a desired outcome or solution.

- Continuing to challenge the brain serves as protection against age-related mental decline and preserves memory and intelligence.

Spiritual Energy

Spiritual energy is derived from a connection to deeply held values and a purpose beyond our self-interest. Spiritual energy is sustained by balancing a commitment to a purpose above and beyond ourselves without neglecting self-care.

- The key "muscle" that serves spiritual energy is character. It can be built by finding systematic ways to expose it to trials and tribulations.

Emotional Energy

In order to perform at our best, we must access pleasant and positive emotions: joy, challenges, adventures, and opportunities.

- The key "muscles" or competencies that fuel positive emotions are self-confidence, self-regulation, empathy, and social skills. We can systematically build our capacities in this system by intermittently exposing them to periods of intensity and recovery.

Physical Energy

Physical energy is the fundamental source of fuel for other energy dimensions, primarily emotional and mental energies.

- Breathing is one of the most important regulators of physical energy. You will benefit from learning to manage your breathing by practicing simple breathing exercises.
- Food and water are important energy sources. Avoid long breaks between meals. Eating five to six low calorie, highly nutritious meals a day insures a steady resupply of energy.
- Other than eating and breathing, sleep is the most important source of recovery. Most adult human beings require seven to eight hours of sleep per night to function optimally.
- Physical exercise produces significant benefits. Interval training with heartrate oscillations is preferable to continuous exercise.

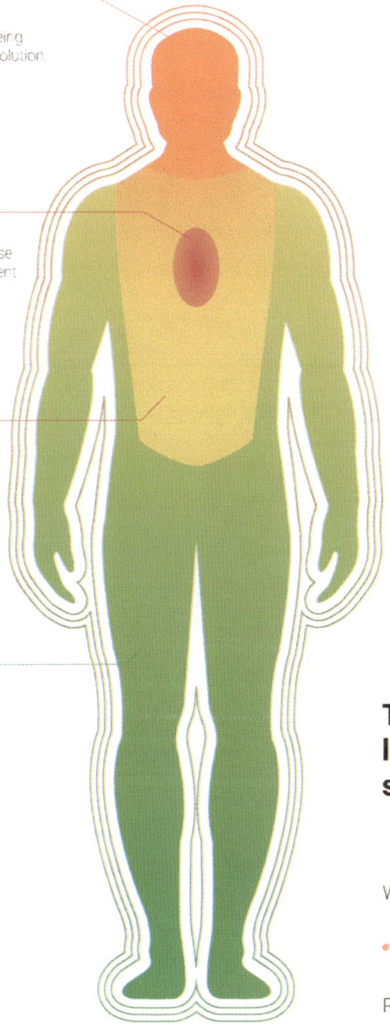

Our physical energy capacity is measured in terms of quantity (low to high) and emotional capacity in quality (negative to positive).

	High Negative	High Positive
	Angry Anxious Fearful Resentful Panicking Defensive	Invigorated Challenged Connected Joyful Confident
	Low Negative	**Low Positive**
	Depressed Exhausted Fearful Burned out Hopeless Defeated	Relaxed Mellow Peaceful Tranquil Serene

PERFORMANCE

To key to being truly effective in our lives is learning how to rhythmically spend and then renew our energy.

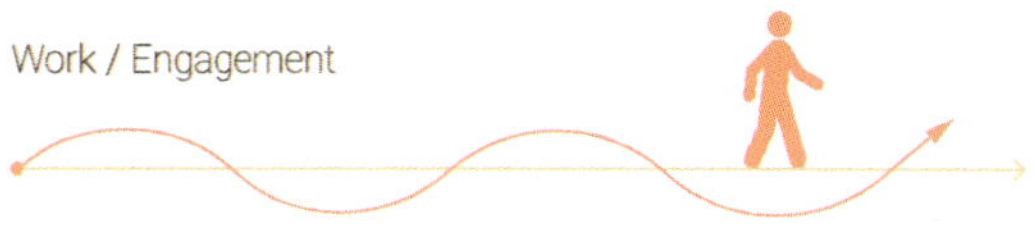

Work / Engagement

Rest / Recovery

The Rules of Engagement

Defining Purpose

Purpose becomes a powerful and enduring source of energy when its source moves:

- From negative to positive
- From external to internal
- From self to others

Facing the Truth

It is one thing to clarify our values and quite another to behave in accordance with them every day. Both are necessary to generate positive energy.

Avoiding the truth consumes great effort and energy in various domains, including physical energy.

Retain ongoing openness to the possibility that you may not be seeing yourself — or others — as you/they truly are.

Creating Positive Rituals

By turning certain actions that can renew our reserves of energy into a ritual, we offset our limited willpower and discipline as these actions now become automatic.

Rituals create a means by which we cement behaviors, make lasting change, set new priorities, and train 'muscles' of all other energy dimensions.

The Blue Zones: Lessons for Living Longer From the People Who've Lived the Longest

Dan Buettner

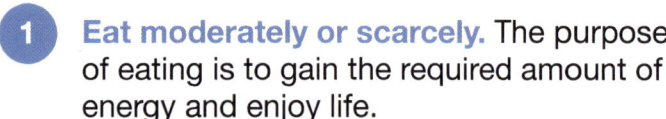

1. **Eat moderately or scarcely.** The purpose of eating is to gain the required amount of energy and enjoy life.

2. **Eat 80 percent of what you have on your plate.** Stop eating as soon as you no longer feel hungry. This will help you stay fit and resist fast-food temptations.

3. **Eat more plant products, don't forget about nuts.** Limit intake of meat, as it may contribute to arteria thrombosis and fat accumulation.

4. **Build activity into your routine and lifestyle.** But don't get obsessed with marathon walks. Moderation is key.

5. **Be in synch with your circadian rhythm.** Get a good night's sleep. The body clock works better when it corresponds to the planet's biorhythms.

6. **Find your purpose.** As long as you feel the urge to do something, you will not let yourself get weaker and die.

7. **Get closer to your family and do your best to make them happy.** You will enjoy taking care of others, and they will help you in a time of need.

8. **Stay connected to the world.** A stranger is a friend we haven't met yet.

9. **Have faith.** Believing means knowing and accepting the wisdom of the world.

10. **Study specifics of your area (geographic or physical properties) and make good use of them.**

The Blue Zones

Dan Buettner

Reaching old age is like a winning lottery ticket. If all the right numbers fall into place a person can live to 100. In this example, winning lottery numbers mean good health, social and eating habits, as well as physical exercise.

EXTERNAL FACTORS
Make good use of your region's geographic properties

Physical isolation
A remote location does have its benefits, as the people there preserve their traditions and pass on their experience.

Geographic properties
Water, terrain, natural resources may become your allies.

Local diet
What do locals in your area consider a source for good health?

Make your lifestyle active
Build activity into your routine and lifestyle. Don't force yourself to do things you dislike.

EATING

Eat moderately
Eat 80 percent of what you have on your plate.

Eat unprocessed foods
Don't give in to fast-food temptations.

Limit your intake of meat, focus on plant products
Meat may contribute to arterial thrombosis and fat accumulation. Focus on grains, beans, nuts, fruit and vegetables.

EXERCISE AND LABOR

Be in synch with your circadian clock
Get a good night's sleep.

Take time to relieve stress
Leave the past behind and enjoy the moment.

Craft a personal mission statement
If you don't have a sense of purpose? Why do you get up in the morning? Centenarians have a reason to live.

SOCIALIZATION AND SPIRITUALITY

Stay connected to the world
A stranger is a friend we haven't met yet.

Put family first
Enjoy taking care of others.

Create time together
It can be the company of friends or people who share the same hobby.

Have faith
Believing means knowing and accepting the wisdom of the world.

People on Okinawa manage to reach the age of 100 at a rate three times higher than Americans do, suffer one-fifth of the number of heart disease issues, and live about seven years longer.

Personal development: 50 bestsellers in infographics

Full Catastrophe Living: Using the Wisdom of Your Body and Mind to Face Stress, Pain, and Illness

Jon Kabatt-Zinn

1. **The first step to healing is mindfulness, which is a particular way of paying attention to things that we have come to ignore while going about our daily routine.**

2. **The meditation process catalyzes the work of healing.** By meditating, you learn to deal with physical and emotional pain.

3. **Self-discipline and regular practice are vital to self-healing.**

4. **Meditation can be practiced at home, at work, or while traveling.** The most important thing is to practice every day, regardless of your mood, schedule, or the way you feel.

5. **Choose a convenient time for meditation, even it you can only spend on it five minutes a day on it.**

6. **It is essential for people to engage in systematic training of the mind, such as practicing mindfulness, to free themselves from the non-stop distorting effect of their daily emotional and thought processes, and to manage stress.**

7. **By doing body scanning, meditation, or yoga, we reestablish contact with our body, learn to read its signals, and regulate its tension.**

8. **If you are having trouble sleeping, it might be because you do not live in the moment when you are awake, but rather are on full autopilot.**

9. **Life is a constant transformation, thereby making stress inevitable.** But we can change the way we perceive stress.

10. **Seven attitudinal factors constitute the major pillars of mindfulness practice.** They are non-judging, patience, having a beginner's mind, trust, non-striving, acceptance, and letting go.

Full Catastrophe Living

Jon Kabatt-Zinn

Psychological factors may either protect or increase a person's susceptibleness to disease. Using mindfulness, we can change our way of thinking and progress on a path toward improved health and healing.

MINDFULNESS PRACTICE

Paying attention to things that we have come to ignore, taking them for granted

Non-judging
Become aware of the constant stream of judgements flowing through you and how you react to inner and outer experiences you are caught up in, and learn to step back from them.

Patience
To be patient is to be completely open to each moment, knowing that things can only unfold in their own timeframe.

Beginner's Mind
Forget about your past experiences! They lead to expectations, judgements, and convictions that prevent us from seeing things as they really are.

Trust
Trust your intuition and your authority over your body. For example, when you practice yoga, listen to your body.

Acceptance
Acceptance means seeing things in the present as they actually are. It is part of the healing process.

Non-striving
Back off from striving for results and start focusing carefully on seeing and accepting things as they are, moment by moment.

Letting Go
Don't hold on to thoughts, affections, feelings, or experiences.

MEDITATION TECHNIQUES

People who practice meditation regularly have greater resilience in the face of stressors and a reduced reaction to stress

Breathing

Mindful breathing is the starting point of the healing process. Focus on breathing and the sensations related to it.

Body Scanning

Lie on your back and move your mind through the different regions of your body. Let your breathing move through your entire body.

Sitting Meditation

In addition to breathing, expand your field of attention to include your body's sensations in particular regions or your entire body, sounds, and finally the thought process itself.

Hatha Yoga
Do gentle stretching and strengthening exercises, but very slowly, with moment-to-moment awareness of your breathing and your body's sensations.

Walking Meditation

Focus on the sensations in your feet and legs, or alternatively, how your whole body feels while in motion.

How Not to Die. Discover the Foods Scientifically Proven to Prevent and Reverse Disease

Michael Greger

1. **There may be no such thing as dying from old age.** People die from disease, and most early deaths are related to what we eat.

2. **People in developed countries live longer now, but they are living fewer healthy years then they once did.**

3. **There are seven simple health components:** not smoking, not being obese, exercising (at least 22 minutes of walking daily), eating more healthfully (a lot of vegetables and fruit); having cholesterol levels below 6.0 mmol/l, maintaining normal blood pressure (120/70 with age-related variations) and normal blood sugar levels (3.3–5.5 mmol/l)

4. **Alcohol consumption, even in moderate amounts, increases the risk of several diseases.** Excessive drinking is defined as the regular consumption of more than one drink a day for women and more than two for men. A drink is defined as five ounces of wine, 12 ounces of beer, or 1.5 ounces of hard liquor.

5. **The top 15 killers are:** coronary heart disease, lung diseases, brain diseases, digestive cancers, infections, diabetes, high blood pressure, liver disease, blood cancers, kidney disease, breast cancer, suicide, prostate cancer, Parkinson's disease, and medical interventions.

6. **Most visits to doctors are for diseases that can be prevented with a healthful diet and lifestyle.**

7. **The more colorful vegetables, fruit, and berries are, the more benefit they provide to your health.** Colorful foods are often more healthful because they contain antioxidant pigments.

8. **Sugar and all artificial and natural sweeteners are harmful.** Only date sugar and blackstrap molasses get the green light in terms of your health.

9. **Supplements are not as good for your health as natural food.** It makes sense to supplement your diet with substances that are not made by plants: vitamin B12, iodine, and vitamin D3 in areas of limited sunlight.

10. **The 12 components that must be present regularly in every person's life are:** beans, berries, fruits, cruciferous vegetables, greens, other vegetables, flaxseeds, nuts, spices, whole grains, water, and exercise.

How Not to Die

Michael Gregor

Most early deaths can be prevented. Our genes account for only 10 to 20 percent of the risk. The main cause of early death is a bad diet.

SOURCES OF HEALTH AND LONGEVITY

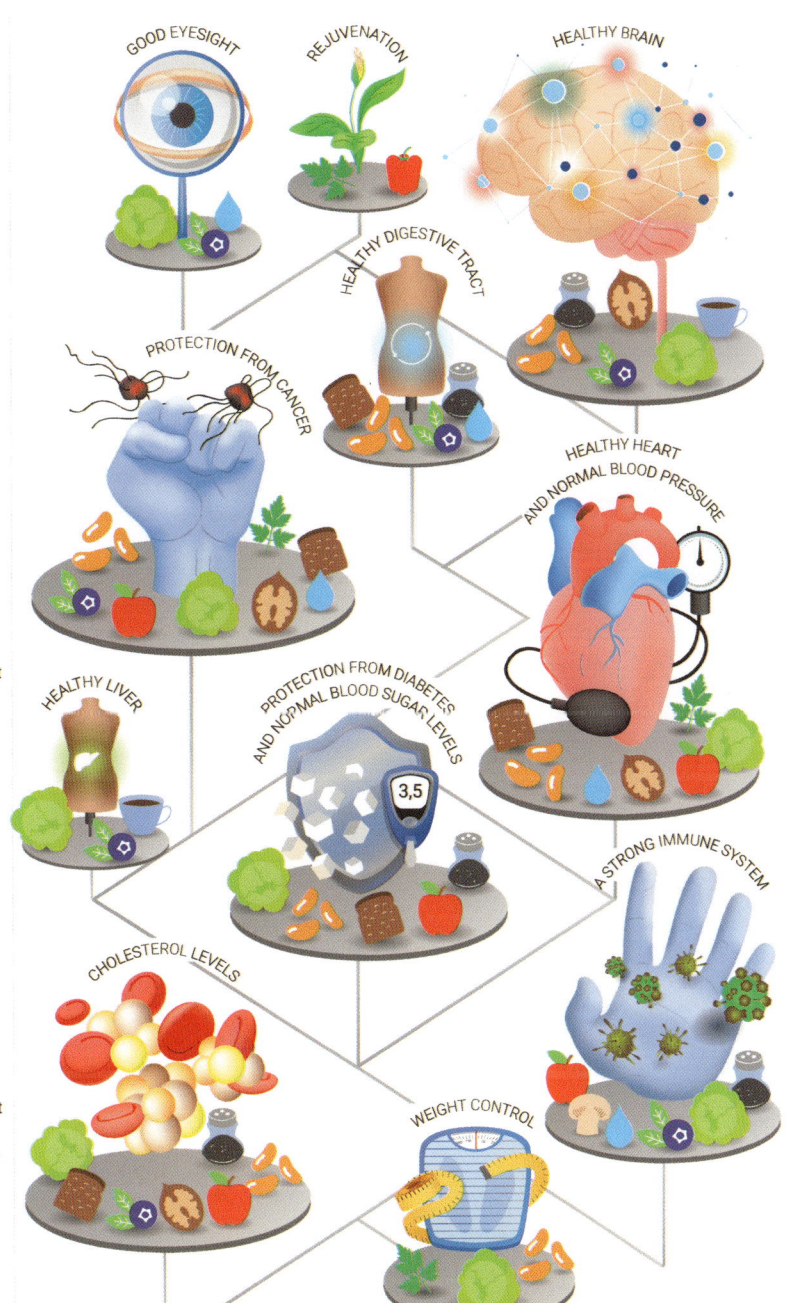

BEANS
- Lower bad cholesterol and blood sugar levels
- Offer potential protection against cancer
- Reduce the risk of heart diseases and strokes

BERRIES
- Offer potential protection against cancer
- Boost the immune system
- Guard the liver, stomach and brain
- Lower cholesterol levels
- Protect against vision loss

OTHER FRUITS
- Boost the immune system
- Lower bad cholesterol and blood sugar levels
- **Kiwifruit** are prescribed for insomnia
- **Citrus** fruit lower the risk of cancer

 ### GREENS
- Reduce the risk of cancer, heart attack and stroke
- Promote regeneration
- Abolish carcinogens
- May help with weight loss

 ### VEGETABLES
- **Red pepper and tomatoes** boost the immune system
- **Tomatoes** decrease the risk of heart attack and stroke
- **Beetroot** regulates blood pressure
- **Carrot, pumpkin, and cabbage** are associated with a lower risk of colon cancer
- **Leeks and garlic** help to prevent lymphoma and breast cancer, offer protection against toxins and diabetes
- **Cruciferous** vegetables help to protect the liver, brain and eyesight

 ### MUSHROOMS
- Boost the immune system
- Have a strong anti-inflammatory effect

NUTS
- Reduce the risk of cardiovascular diseases
- Drop bad cholesterol levels
- Help to protect the brain

 ### SPICES
- **Turmeric** has a strong anti-inflammatory effect and boosts the immune system
- **Coriander** offers protection for your joints
- **Cayenne** pepper and ginger are used for headaches
- **Cinnamon** drops blood sugar levels

 ### WHOLE GRAINS
Reduce the risk of:
- Cardiovascular diseases
- Type II diabetes
- Obesity and strokes
- Stomach diseases

Flaxseeds reduce the risk of hypertension, breast cancer and prostate cancer.

 ### BEVERAGES
Normal daily intake: 1.8 l
- **Water** decreases the risks of fractures, heart diseases, lung diseases, kidney diseases, bladder cancer, and cataract, boosts the immune system, relieves symptoms of constipation
- **Coffee** protects the liver and brain, but boosts blood pressure levels
- **Tea** (green, black, white) may protect against fungous diseases and breast cancer
- **Hibiscus tea** lowers blood pressure and has an anti-inflammatory effect

 ### EXERCISE
Weight control, prevention of cardiovascular diseases, reduction of blood sugar levels

At least 22 minutes of walking daily

HEALTHFUL LIFESTYLE

 Not smoking
 Having cholesterol levels below average
 Exercising
 Having normal blood pressure
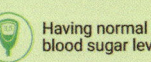 Not being obese
Having normal blood sugar levels
 Eating a lot of vegetables and fruit
 Having at least seven hours of sleep a night

Personal development: 50 bestsellers in infographics

The Telomere Effect: A Revolutionary Approach to Living Younger, Healthier, Longer

Elizabeth Blackburn, Elissa Epel

1. **If you want to look younger than your age, take good care of your telomeres.** Simple lifestyle changes as described below will affect your telomere upkeep within four months.

2. **Treat stress as a challenge.** For example, tell yourself, "Stress energizes me so that I can deal properly with this problem."

3. **Temper negative styles of thinking, such as hostility, mind wandering, pessimism, rumination, and thought suppression.**

4. **Take a telomere trajectory self-test to see where your telomeres need the most help, and gradually affect the changes you'd like to make.**

5. **Do exercises regularly.** For example, go jogging for 45 minutes three times a week, alternating between going quickly and slowly.

6. **Get enough sleep.**

7. **Be a sensitive parent and teach your children how to cope with stress, instead of protecting them from potential disappointments.** Ask them questions, don't order them around.

8. **Instead of dieting by restricting calories, cut down on sugary foods and reduce overeating.**

9. **Maintain a good level of social cohesion: live with those who love you, create your own cozy place, and make friends with your neighbors.**

10. **Improve your educational level and try to earn enough money from your intellectual labor to at least meet your basic needs.**

The Telomere Effect

Elizabeth Blackburn (Nobel Prize winner), Elissa Epel

The main cause of aging is the shortening of telomeres, which are the lighter regions at the end of chromosomes in every human body cell. The condition of your telomeres and the entire body can be significantly improved.

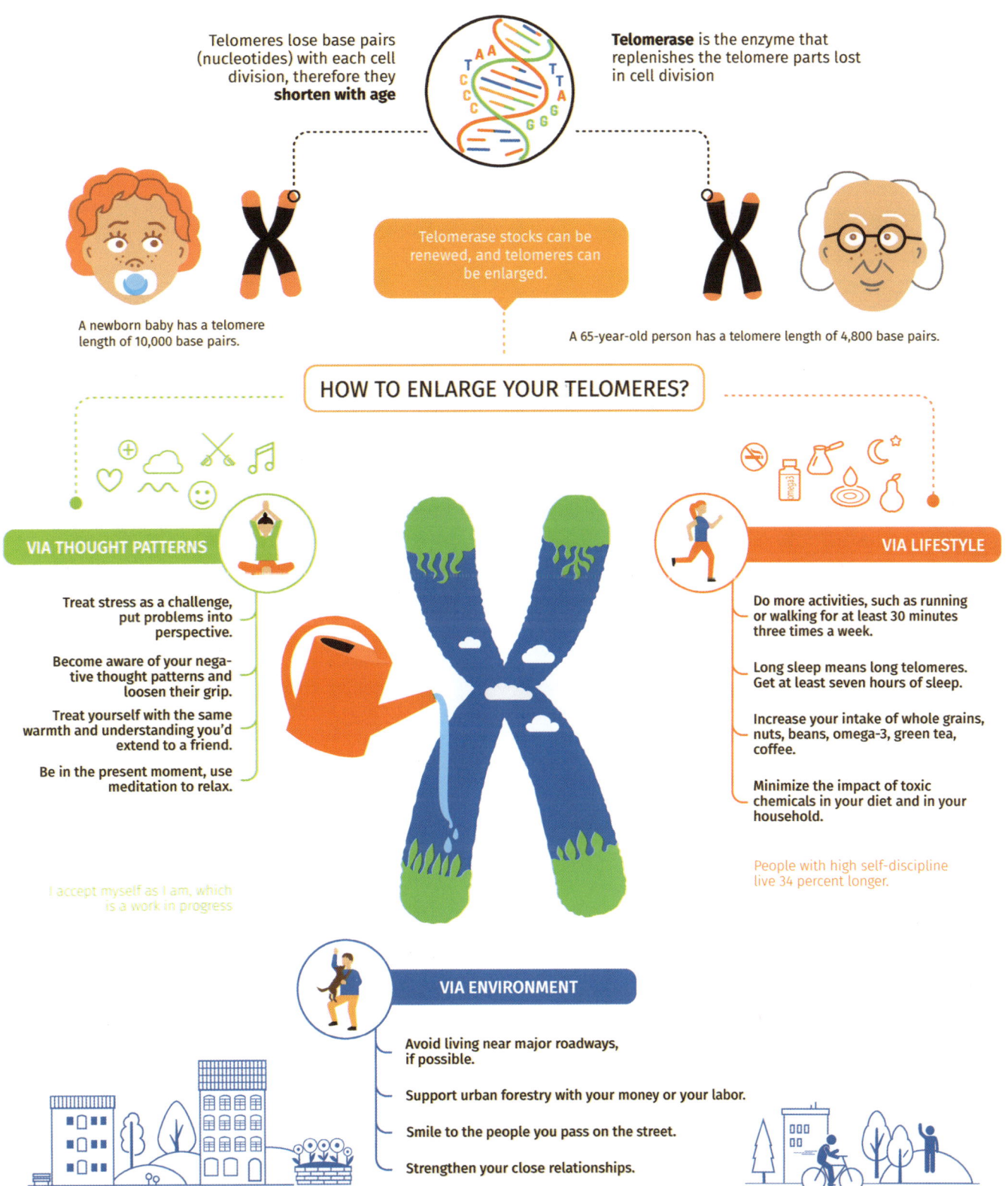

Telomeres lose base pairs (nucleotides) with each cell division, therefore they **shorten with age**

Telomerase is the enzyme that replenishes the telomere parts lost in cell division

Telomerase stocks can be renewed, and telomeres can be enlarged.

A newborn baby has a telomere length of 10,000 base pairs.

A 65-year-old person has a telomere length of 4,800 base pairs.

HOW TO ENLARGE YOUR TELOMERES?

VIA THOUGHT PATTERNS

- Treat stress as a challenge, put problems into perspective.
- Become aware of your negative thought patterns and loosen their grip.
- Treat yourself with the same warmth and understanding you'd extend to a friend.
- Be in the present moment, use meditation to relax.

I accept myself as I am, which is a work in progress

VIA LIFESTYLE

- Do more activities, such as running or walking for at least 30 minutes three times a week.
- Long sleep means long telomeres. Get at least seven hours of sleep.
- Increase your intake of whole grains, nuts, beans, omega-3, green tea, coffee.
- Minimize the impact of toxic chemicals in your diet and in your household.

People with high self-discipline live 34 percent longer.

VIA ENVIRONMENT

- Avoid living near major roadways, if possible.
- Support urban forestry with your money or your labor.
- Smile to the people you pass on the street.
- Strengthen your close relationships.

Personal development: 50 bestsellers in infographics

The Oxygen Advantage: Simple, Scientifically Proven Breathing Techniques to Help You Become Healthier, Slimmer, Faster, and Fitter

Patrick McKeown

1. **Habitual over-breathing involves more air than your body requires during rest and exercise.** Over-breathing leads to a reduction of carbon dioxide in the blood.

2. **Carbon dioxide allows the release of oxygen from red blood cells;** if we exhale too much carbon dioxide, we supply less oxygen to our muscles and organs.

3. **Having a greater tolerance to carbon dioxide allows for much more effective supply of oxygen to your working muscles during exercise,** which improves endurance and allows you to achieve better performance at sports with less effort.

4. **It is very important to breathe through your nose day and night.**

5. **Nasal breathing is imperative for harnessing the benefits of nitric oxide,** which, among other things, helps prevent high blood pressure.

6. **Correct breathing, which is abdominal breathing,** involves the proper use of the diaphragm, and improves the performance of the lymphatic system.

7. **Breath-holding exercises may simulate high-altitude training,** which increases red blood cell count and, respectively, improves oxygen supply to the muscles.

8. **To win a competition, learn to reduce unnecessary thought activity, concentrate on your breathing and enter a zone where the body and mind merge together.**

9. **Breath-holding exercises provide the best protection against oxidative stress.**

10. **Correct breathing helps us lose weight and gives us protection against heart diseases and asthma.**

The Oxygen Advantage

Patrick McKeown

We unconsciously breathe in two to three times more air than we need. Correct breathing makes us healthier and helps improve our fitness and endurance.

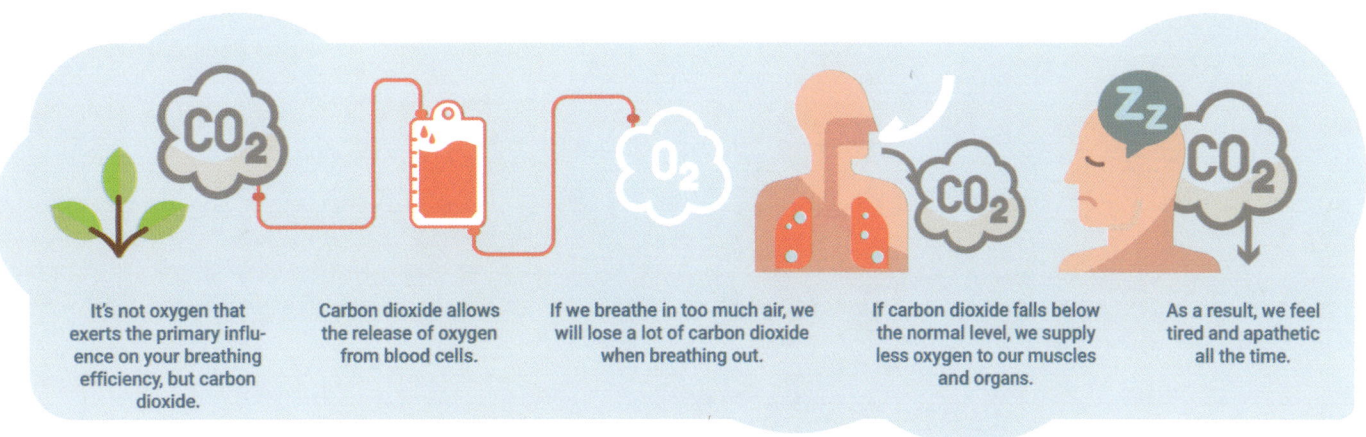

It's not oxygen that exerts the primary influence on your breathing efficiency, but carbon dioxide.

Carbon dioxide allows the release of oxygen from blood cells.

If we breathe in too much air, we will lose a lot of carbon dioxide when breathing out.

If carbon dioxide falls below the normal level, we supply less oxygen to our muscles and organs.

As a result, we feel tired and apathetic all the time.

HOW TO BREATHE CORRECTLY

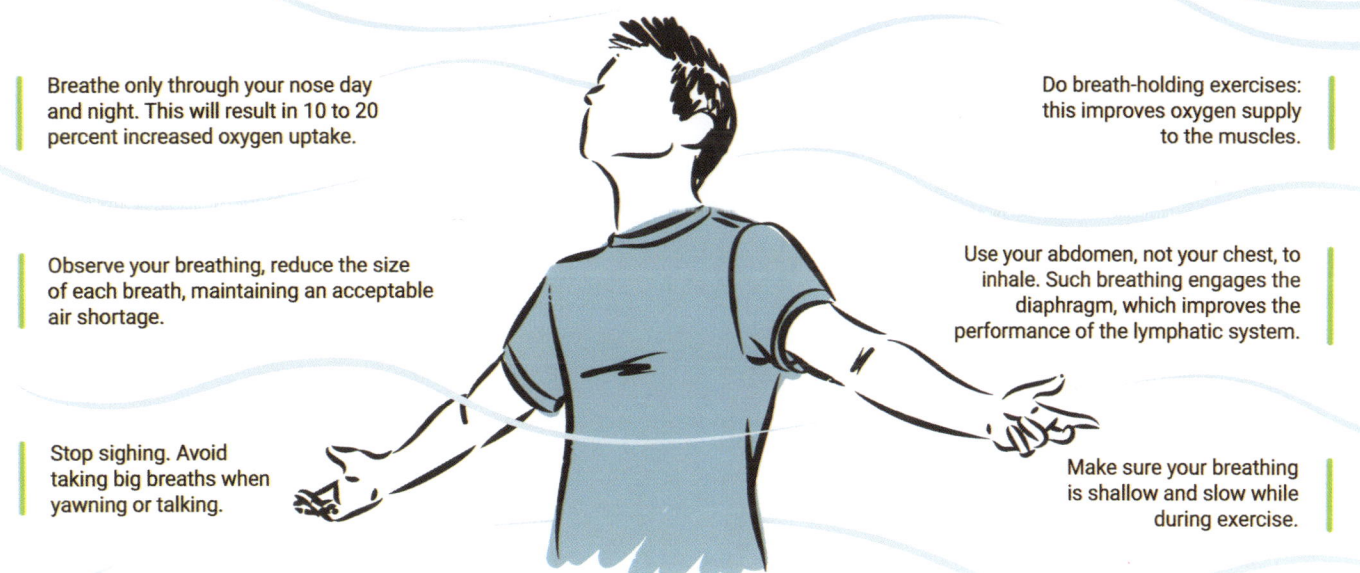

Breathe only through your nose day and night. This will result in 10 to 20 percent increased oxygen uptake.

Observe your breathing, reduce the size of each breath, maintaining an acceptable air shortage.

Stop sighing. Avoid taking big breaths when yawning or talking.

Do breath-holding exercises: this improves oxygen supply to the muscles.

Use your abdomen, not your chest, to inhale. Such breathing engages the diaphragm, which improves the performance of the lymphatic system.

Make sure your breathing is shallow and slow while during exercise.

BODY OXYGEN LEVEL TEST (BOLT): THE LENGTH OF TIME YOU CAN COMFORTABLY GO WITHOUT INHALING AFTER EXHALING

A perfect score. The natural pause between each breath is about 4 to 5 seconds

40 seconds

A common score for people who exercise regularly

20 seconds

Loss of carbon dioxide, oxygen level reduction in muscles, vessel and air passage constriction

less than 20 seconds

**Personal development:
50 bestsellers in infographics**

Prepared by Ivi Green
hello@ivigreen.com

Printed in Great Britain
by Amazon